Published by Robert Deaves

First Edition 2018

Copyright © Robert Deaves, 2018

ISBN: 978-0-9559001-8-1

chrOniKle

Celebrating 60 Years of the OK Dinghy

Compiled and edited by Robert Deaves

CONTENTS

PART 2 – Sailors and Boats

▶ ▶ ▶

FOREWORD

To celebrate 60 years of sailing OK Dinghies, Robert Deaves had the idea for a book of sailors' stories. For most of the last 60 years the OK Dinghy class has had a reputation not just for high quality, world class sailing, but for a world renowned social side which has attracted great friends from many countries. This book celebrates the stories of the people from the OK community  when the main story was not what happened on the water, but what happened after in the bar or at the party to follow. These stories now move from myth to legend.

I have been fortunate to read a draft of the book and it makes compelling reading. Stories from before my time and others during, that I am fascinated to read for the first time. I have also shared a story of my trip to Europe in 1985 with fellow Australians Roger Blasse, Neil Williamson and Peter Milne, two of whom have gone on to win World Championships – in Roger's case twice. But more importantly, the spirit of the OK class is such that more than 30 years later, we are still good friends both in and around OK sailing.

I would like to thank Robert for his drive, passion and sheer hard work to bring this project from concept to reality. You are a tremendous asset to the OK class and sailing in general. Also, I would like to thank everyone who took the time to write down their stories for all the world to read, share and perhaps embellish a little further as time goes on.

I look forward to creating and sharing many more great stories over the next 60 years.

Mark Jackson
President OKDIA

INTRODUCTION

ANYONE WHO HAS EVER SAILED an OK Dinghy will almost certainly have spent a long evening at a sailing club bar somewhere in the world listening to stories of events past, of hilarious trips and experiences and the often-dubious activities of some sailors. Some of these stories seem quite fanciful, some have been embellished over the years, many inevitably involve alcohol and some cannot be published for legal reasons, but all have become compelling legends of the class.

Throughout 2017, contributions for this volume were requested under a working title of *Project 60*, an initiative to encourage as many people as possible to contribute an anecdote, a funny story or a defining moment for them in the class. We ended up with about 100 individual pieces in this book, of about a diverse a nature as it is possible to collect, from the very earliest days of the class right up to modern times.

Many of the stories included are new tellings of old tales, and these have been supplemented by digging into the OKDIA archives and extracting various key moments from class history. The book opens with the meeting that established the international association and sets the basis for the growth of the class into what was in the early 1970s claimed to be the largest dinghy class in the world.

The stories also include contemporary writings for the class's 60th anniversary in 2017, as well as contributions from sailors past and present about their memories in the class, and what it has meant to them. Various pieces that have been previously published over the years have also been included to document important events and milestones in the history of the class. Some of the pieces are contemporary to the time they were written, so need to be read in that context.

The book has turned into something of a scrapbook of OK Dinghy memories past and present. Its many contributors have painted an alternative picture of the class that is as much a part of its history as the battles that took place on the water.

One of the great periods in OK Dinghy history was the 1980s, when groups of sailors from New Zealand and Australia would venture to Europe for a summer of sailing, and many stories of these legendary 'tours' have been told for the first time in the pages.

Very few of the stories within this volume are stories about the actual racing. There is good reason for that. The 2008 book *Completely OK* covered that in enough detail, so there is no need to repeat those texts. But the class has another aspect that is one of the reasons why it has been so successful for so long: its social and community competence. You will find most of the stories told within these pages concerns a group of characters that loved having fun together, racing together and socialising together, and doing so without a care as to what others thought.

There were also a lot of great stories that did not make this book, good ideas that faded away, unfulfilled promises, or perhaps just a second thought about telling an incriminating tale. If in reading these tales you are prompted to retell your own OK story then please do not hesitate. If enough material surfaces, there will always be room for it in 'chrOniKle Volume 2' at some point in the not too distant future.

In the meantime, enjoy this collection, this scrapbook of everything OK. It is the stuff of legends...

⏩ ⏩ ⏩

SIXTY YEARS OF THE OK DINGHY

THE OK DINGHY WAS THE brainchild of Danish architect Axel
Damgaard Olsen. By 1956, he had already introduced the now
world famous Optimist dinghy into Europe after spotting fleets of them
sailing in Florida, realising their potential and bringing the design home
to Denmark, but for the OK Dinghy, it all started as a vision of a light
fast planning dinghy that could be built and sailed by amateurs, both
quickly and cheaply.

Damgaard was one of a number of Danish Pirat sailors (a German
designed two man boat), who saw the need for a simple fast single
handed dinghy with an unstayed simple rig. He provided the necessary
inspiration for his friend, the Danish yacht designer and boat builder
Knud Olsen, to transfer these ideas to paper. Knud drew the plans for
the first OK Dinghy and the great Finn sailor Paul Elvstrøm helped to
develop the Pirat's somewhat stiff mast into the characteristic bend of
the OK Dinghy mast using his experience in the Finn class.

Although they initially wanted to call the boat a 'KO', using Olsen's
reversed initials this means cow in Danish, so they reversed the letters to
make OK. The first prototype was built during the summer of 1956 and
trial sailed later that year. During the winter of 1956-57 about 70 boats
were built in Denmark and these began racing at several clubs in 1957.
The OK Dinghy was born.

This simple design filled a niche in Denmark at that time, where the
major fleets were the German designed Pirat dinghy, the Snipe and the
Finn. Its single hard chine and relatively flat bottom panels were ideal

for home construction. The original wooden spars and cotton sails could also be constructed by the amateur if local access to sail makers and spar makers was limited. And that is exactly what happened. In garages and sheds right across the world OK Dinghies were carefully put together from a set of plans supplied from Knud Olsen in Denmark.

In the early days the boat was considered to be dangerous in Denmark and several race committees tried to have it banned because it kept capsizing too much. Most of the sailors in the class at that time came from keelboats, so were unused to the unstable OK Dinghy and spent considerable time upside down. However people such as Elvstrøm and others gave the boat their vote of confidence and gradually the sailors became more proficient. The OK Dinghy was described as being "like a mustang, a wild horse, compared to a Finn dinghy which was than like a domesticated horse."

In the years that followed enthusiasts across the world picked up on Axel Damgaard's vision and Knud Olsen's neat little design and set about buying plans and building boats. Over the coming decade, the class spread to France, Sweden, Australia, New Zealand, USA, Canada, Japan, Zambia, Norway, Poland, Kenya, Pakistan, India, Finland, Thailand, South Africa, Barbados, Belgium, Switzerland, the UK, Germany, Italy, Morocco, Portugal, Rhodesia, Tasmania and many other places. Until the mid-1970s the class continued to grow at a phenomenal rate worldwide, when the introduction of the Laser put the brakes on production in some countries.

In 1962 the OK Dinghy International Association was established after a meeting of sailors in Holland. Sven Hornewall from Norway became the first President while Basil Crosby from the UK, who was also secretary of the British OK Dinghy Association at the time, became the first secretary of OKDIA. The first World Championship was held the following summer in Maubuisson in France.

Axel Damgaard was the driving force in these early days. His enthusiasm for the class enabled it to grow and become the global success story it is today. He encouraged builders to keep everything simple and fun. The simple plywood construction lent itself perfectly to home construction and the self-sufficient home builder is still very much part of the class today as they were 60 years ago.

⏩ ⏩ ⏩

PART I
A Scrapbook of OK Stories

Where it all Started

This is the document that begins the history of OKDIA. It takes up the first pages of the OKDIA Minute Book and is titled: 'Memorandum of the discussion in 1962 at Veerse Meer on the formation of an OK Dinghy International Association.

A NUMBER OF US WENT TO the International Regatta at Veerse Meer on September 1st and 2nd 1962, enjoyed some very agreeable racing and had a series of discussions on the future development of the OK from the international point of view, and also on the possibility of forming an international organisation. This followed a correspondence between a number of us, which had suggested we were all thinking along the same lines and that now was the time for action.

In these discussions at Veerse Meer the following countries were represented.

Belgium, represented by Alphonse Haverhals

France, by Hubert Lepicard (Aspryok) & Gilbert Grou-Radenez

Germany, by Gottfried Dehncke

Great Britain, by Roger Stiles & Basil Crosby

Norway, by Sven Hornewall (A memorandum representing the Norwegian's point of view written by Olé With was also submitted by a Norwegian visitor.)

Sweden, by Sven Hornewall

It was unanimously decided to form an international association to promote and assist in the development of the OK Dinghy and to stimulate the growth of fleets throughout the world, and to encourage by every means, international racing in the class. All those present at the discussion were unanimous in wishing to see the class attain international status and recognition by the IYRU. It was proposed to submit an application for this not later than August 1963.

Sven Hornewall was asked to accept the presidency of the new association and he agreed to undertake this, and Basil Crosby was asked and agreed to undertake the secretaryship for three years. It was proposed that the Secretary should retire at the expiration of three years of office and that in the interests of continuity, the retirement of President and Secretary should not coincide.

On the all important question of rules, it was decided to adopt the British rules as a basis. These could be modified to meet the wishes of other national associations, where there was a firm majority for any particular modification. Part one was approved in its entirety. It was agreed that the British would modify their headboard to conform to the Scandinavian pattern with an equivalent of 150mm sides.

A discussion followed on the sheerguard. The French enlarge a part of this between frames, to a section that would lie within a square of 50 mm to limit the discomfort felt on vigorous sitting out. In deference to the strong French wishes it was thought that this should be tried out before a decision was reached, and it is hoped that arrangements will be made by other National Associations to do this.

It was hoped that consideration be given to a centre of gravity test like the one the Finn class uses.

Everyone agreed that, simplicity, cheapness, and as little rules changing as possible were the principles that should always be kept in mind when considering development.

On the subject of finance, it was proposed that the association be supported by a subscription from member associations of the equivalent of 2/6d per each registered boat.

An international championship will be held, probably at Maubuisson in July next year and it was hoped that a training camp could be run in conjunction with this event. The Olympic basis of scoring would be used. There would be seven races in five days. A suitable trophy will have to be found. It was proposed that for this and indeed other events a rule could be introduced restricting one mast and one sail to each boat.

During this and subsequent international championships the Annual General Meeting of the association would be held and the business of the class transacted.

Entries for the Saturday meeting would close two weeks before the event.

It was recognised that the International Association would have to run a newsletter publishing its activities. The Secretary was asked to prepare some proposals.

The action to be taken following this meeting was to include the preparation of a memo of the discussion (now submitted), the circulation of al National and would-be National Associations of this memo inviting their support. The President and Secretary to prepare a draft constitution to submit to the National Association and the beginning to be made on the final draft of the International Rules. And finally, some preparation made for a submission to the IYRU of an application for recognition of the OK as an international class.

Going Home Like Vikings – Per Westlund

The first world championship in the OK Dinghy was organised by Cercle de la Voile de Bordeaux in 1963. Per Westlund was sailing S 60 at that time, today he is still sailing, in SWE 2815

I WAS 18 YEARS OLD AND had been enrolled in the mandatory military service in the Swedish army for a month. The officers had no understanding of sailing so I had to fight hard to get permission to leave. The fact that I was ruling Swedish champion in the OK Dinghy finally convinced them to give me the permission for 14 days. Wow, the last obstacle was eliminated, I thought.

In order to drive from Sweden to Bordeaux with two boats on our trailer I had convinced my father to let me borrow his Volvo Amazon and I had taken the driver's license. At the same time I was preparing for my baccalaureate and it was necessary to get top marks to be admitted to the Institute of Technology where I wanted to study. It was a very busy spring filled with dreams and ambitions.

I took my exam and the next day I began my military service. From day one in the military I had to work hard to get a permission to leave for the World Championship in Maubuisson. Finally everything was arranged, but five days before the departure from Sweden I got a serious throat infection and a very high fever. I was placed in the military hospital for treatment. It felt like a prison when the doctor said that my recovery would take seven to 10 days. My efforts to convince him to let me go were in vain. He frankly said, "I will not let you go. This is serious and you can go sailing another year." The only remaining way for me was to try to convince the nurses. My plan was to bring down the fever a little step-by-step every day by manipulation of the fever thermometer. So I did and the fever curve looked better and better. In the morning when my permission to leave started, the thermometer showed 37 centigrade. I was scared they would check me closer as my true fever was far too high. The nurse looked me into my eyes and said, "I cannot stop you and I will let you go even if I know that you are far from recovered."

My co-driving friends had loaded the trailer with our boats and waited outside the military camp. I stumbled through the gates, rushed into the car and told them. "Go before they catch me."

It took three days to drive down to Bordeaux and out to Maubuisson and I was sleeping in the back seat all the way down, but finally I was back to health again.

Maubuisson was a charming little tourist village with some restaurants and a camping ground with sandy beaches at Lac de Lacanau. Some 60 boats participated from France, UK, Denmark, Holland, Belgium, Norway and Sweden.

The races started and I won the first one and I also won the second race. Being fully recovered from the fever, the winner of the first two races, on my first travel abroad without parents and free from the hardships in the military service I was up in the sky. Late nights at the bar La Pergola, wine, new friends and cute girls were maybe too much distraction for a young guy. The third race didn't go so well and I lost my lead. Finally I ended up as number five. Fair enough, I could go home with pride and a lot of experiences.

Svend Jakobsen was the winner. He sailed well and maybe he handled the local temptations better than I did.

Before our departure from this lovely place it was time for the prize-giving ceremony. The club, Cercle de Voile de Bordeaux, seemed to be the meeting place for the owners of the wine estates in the region. They were dressed in black jackets and tie. The ceremony went on in the normal way and we all got generous gifts of wine and liquor from the most famous chateaux in the region. When they turned to me and handed over the bottles, our Swedish team leader, Sven Hornewall, who also was the President of OKDIA, stepped forward and asked for silence. He told the audience in perfect French that it was great to get all those prizes but unfortunately this young guy couldn't accept any alcoholic products because he was member of a sailing club named Nykterhetsvännernas Segel Sällskap, meaning the Sailing Club for Soberness. True, that was

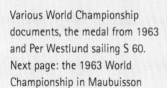

Various World Championship documents, the medal from 1963 and Per Westlund sailing S 60. Next page: the 1963 World Championship in Maubuisson

the odd name but it was not exactly what I wanted to hear now. It was like a frozen moment and the race officers got embarrassed and rushed into the clubhouse to find a solution. After what seemed to be an eternity they came out smiling and took back the bottles from me and handed over a gold plated medal of The Chamber of Commerce in Bordeaux. All smiles again. Our team leader Sven Hornevall stepped forward a second time and prized the solution but suggested that my family would be very happy to get some gifts from this famous wine region and I could be the ambassador for the Bordeaux area. So finally I got all bottles back and all of us were more than happy with the outcome.

We could go home like the old Vikings with booty of wine, gold and victories.

The wine is gone, but the medal is on my prize shelf and the warm memories of the first worlds in the OK Dinghy are alive.

'Ping Pong' and Hugh Patton – Mike Patton

'Ping Pong' was the first British built OK Dinghy, owned by Hugh Patton, sometime Chairman of the British OK Dinghy Association

MY DAD HAS ALWAYS BEEN around boats since his teens. Originally with an International 14 at Broadstairs in Kent, and then on the Isle of Wight. He was one of the founder members of the Island Sailing Club, whilst earning his livelihood at Whites shipbuilders as a draughtsman.

After the war, a wife and children precluded him from his first love, boats, Then around 1957 he was messing about in the back of his watch and clock shop in Bath. He set about drawing the outline of a boat. At this time we knew nothing of boating, but coincidently it the birth date of this fabulous dinghy. It must have been in his psyche even then.

He bought a kit from the Bell Woodworking Co of Southampton GP14 number 911. She was eventually finished later in the year, and launched at the Bristol Avon Sailing Club. Such was the build quality of 'Diamond', it wasn't long before he was taking orders. He set up his boat-building department and things took off.

He travelled around the UK to various open meetings, and competed pretty successfully during 1957 and 1958. However, it was becoming more and more difficult to get a regular crew; my brother and I were too young.

By this time Dad had built many varied boats alongside his beloved GP14s. British Moth, Heron, 505, And his biggest challenge, a Shearwater catamaran.

Early in 1959, we had travelled to Christchurch to compete in their regatta, where we sailed out from Mudeford. A very good friend of the family had a caravan here and we were using it as a base. Whilst putting 'Diamond' to bed for the evening in the dinghy park, we saw this rather flash white singlehander with a red sail. It turned out to 'Faith', K 7. Dad caught sight of this rather smart thing, and thought this could solve his crewing problems in one fell swoop. Dad walked down towards where the owner was about to beach. Of course it was Richard Creagh-Osborne of Finn fame, ironically with the same number, K 7. They struck up quite a relationship and from this first meeting the first British built OK Dinghy, 'Ping Pong' was born.

Creagh-Osborne had suggested that we register as K 15 to let others know that there were more than just the two boats.

Things were a little hazy over the next couple of years. I spent most of my sailing in a Cadet, during which time Dad had been traveling around the country, competing at various open meetings, and in the early 1960s joined forces with Basil Crosby of Frensham Pond Sailing Club which had a growing fleet of OK Dinghies. The British OK Dinghy Association was formed, and Dad was Chairman for a couple of years

I joined the Merchant Navy as an apprentice pilot in 1962, and I have to admit my sailing took a back seat. During this time Dad had built a number of boats for friends at Lilliput. One of these was his second, named 'Breeze' K 157. Quite a fleet was now building up in the Poole area.

In 1963 the Olympic trials were held by the Royal Motor Club off

Left: A very early picture of Ping Pong taken off Lilliput Sailing Club, in her original varnished hull.

Above right: Hugh Patton reunited at the Maritime Museum Falmouth about 2010. A very emotional day was had by all.

Below: Ping Pong racing in the UK.

Bournemouth, in Studland Bay. Dad was successful in winning this event and had the class been chosen for the Tokyo Olympics, who knows what this would have meant for Dad and the class.

Around 1964 to 1965 Dad had built quite a few more OK Dinghies, including another for himself, he sold 'Breeze' as she wasn't to his liking, and he now had 'Ping Pong II' K 557. It is worth noting at this juncture the similarity in numbers, He only had to add one number to use the same sail from boat to boat. 15, 157, 557.

By 1966 I was back into the fold and started to travel around with Dad and compete in 'Ping Pong', culminating in 1968 when I started to beat him. One notable occasion was at the Swanage Regatta, where I have to say thrashed them all by taking a long beat out to sea, well away from the fleet, found some wind, and managed to plane my way back to win by a country mile.

In 1968 Dad surprisingly sold both OK Dinghies, and bought his first cabin cruiser, a 19-foot Mystic called 'Malin'. He continued to cruise around Poole in a number of different boats, around his beloved Isle of Wight, Guernsey and France, until his late 80s. He reluctantly relinquished the ownership of his last boat, 'Kittywake' to his nephew, also named Hugh by the way. He still spent some time with him right up to his passing on New Year's Day 2013, at the ripe old age of 92.

Paul Elvstrøm and the Early Days of the OK Dinghy

MANY STORIES HAVE BEEN TOLD about the great Paul Elvstrøm. His little known impact on the OK Dinghy was significant, and many believe without his influence the class would have never gained a foothold in Denmark, which eventually led to the gaining of international status. Svend Jakobsen, the first OK Dinghy World Champion in 1963, told this story.

"Paul was a committed supporter of the OK from the very beginning in 1956. He made the first rig and sail that was tested on Axel Damgaard's home water in Vordingborg. The sail had very long battens, but it did not satisfy Knud Olsen and Axel Damgaard (see pictures over). Therefore the mainsail of the Pirat dinghy was chosen instead.

There is no doubt that Paul was consulted all the way until the final choice of rig was agreed, even though it would have been better for his business to choose a new sail/rig.

To support the class Paul accepted to be elected the first chairman of the Danish OK Dinghy Association in the Spring of 1957. He also accepted to be chairman of the Racing Committee at the two first Danish Championships, which was something that he never did for any other classes at that time. He even invited his good friend, Pierre Poulain, a leading Finn helmsman from France, to participate in the first championship. Pierre finished third in a light wind regatta.

To understand the importance of Paul's support we have to remember that many leading officers of the largest yacht clubs in Denmark were dead against the OK Dinghy, and wanted it banned from all racing. The reason for this was that in the junior sailing clubs the mantra was, that if you capsize, you stay with the boat until help arrives. However, the OK Dinghy was a boat that did not fill with water when capsized, but could easily be righted. But in extreme cases there was a risk that the helmsman could not swim to the boat, and that it could drift away.

First sail designs for the
OK Dinghy, by Paul Elvstrøm

Today it seems odd that the most resistance came from Paul's own club, Hellerup. This resulted in a situation where none or only a few OKs were based in Hellerup, something that has certainly changed today. The last 'attack' on the OK came as late as 1962, but after that the resistance disappeared. Today Hellerup is home to one of the largest and most successful fleets of OK Dinghies across the world.

Paul argued all the time for the OK, asserting that nothing was wrong with boat, but the helmsmen had to learn how to sail such a light and demanding boat. As most of the new helmsmen came from heavier dinghies (for example, the Pirat) or the small keelboat (Juniorboat), this would take some time. He also argued, that if the same helmsmen sailed the Finn, the situation would be worse, due to the lack of buoyancy in the Finn that time. His support cannot be overestimated; it was of extreme importance during those years.

Finally Paul took the drawings of the OK Dinghy with him to regattas all over Europe, and convinced his Finn colleagues to introduce the OK Dinghy in their own countries. These included Pierre Poulain in France, Richard Creagh-Osborne in UK, and André Nelis in Belgium. These three countries, together with Scandinavia, were first to get the OK Dinghy going, thanks to Paul."

In fact the founding members of OKDIA came from Belgium, France, Germany, Great Britain, Norway and Sweden. Ironically there was no representative from Denmark at that first meeting.

To recognize the influence of Paul Elvstrøm on the history of the OK Dinghy, even though he never raced the boat, in 2012 he was inducted into the OKDIA Hall of Fame.

Thanks for the Memories – Jan Tyler

OVER THE YEARS BILL AND I gained so many wonderful friends, both here in Australia and overseas. Bill first started sailing OK Dinghies in 1971 and he continued sailing until February 2015 just prior to his diagnosis of Multiple Myeloma, which claimed his life in December 2016.

He took part in numerous regattas, state championships, national championships and world championships over that time. I think you could say he was passionate about sailing OK Dinghies. He didn't win a lot, but that wasn't what it was all about. It was the fun and sheer exhilaration of sailing with his OK buddies that kept him going, and of course the 'post mortem' after every race, downed with a beer – or two – or more. Bill seemed to remember the details of every leg of every race over the years and they were always something for discussion.

He filled many administrative positions over time and he felt a great sense of achievement whilst organising the worlds in Belmont in 2006. He was absolutely overwhelmed when he was inducted into the OKDIA Hall of Fame during the Worlds in Warneműnde, Germany in 2008 – the first Australian to be nominated.

Our home was home to many a visiting OK Dinghy sailor and there was always a bed at the Tylers, even if it was the lounge or the floor. I've lost count how many sailors from around the world stayed with us en route to a regatta or championship, but Bill's hospitality and thorough commitment to the OK fraternity was amazing.

I too enjoyed the camaraderie of the sailors' wives and partners and while the boys were sailing, we always made the most of being together by sharing meals and sightseeing when in different places in the world. Sometimes we got carried away with our social activities and ended up in the bad books when we drove up late to the boat park well after the end of racing. I still remember a few of the boys lying on the grass waiting for us to return so they could access all their clothes and gear that of course was in the car we'd taken out for the day.

I have relayed only a few stories for this book, but there are so many more. If Bill hadn't gone to sailing heaven, he would have had so many tales and stories to tell. He loved nothing more than tapping away with two fingers on his keyboard to write anything about OK Dinghies and the camaraderie of the men who sailed them. Thank you all for the wonderful memories. And thank you Robert Deaves for the opportunity to allow us to relay our stories.

Extracts from the First OKDIA Newsletter – 1965

OUR FIRST INTERNATIONAL NEWSLETTER WAS planned to tell you about the outstanding event in the OK calendar the World Championship and it was also intended to report, what can now be seen as one of the non events of the racing dinghy calendar, the IYRU One Man Boat Trials at Weymouth. Both these events are reported at some length in these columns. We also report the Cairns Green Island ocean race, outstanding in an astonishing example of enterprise and initiative by the organizers – who seem to have their own magic carpet.

But first a glance at the Class, its distribution, and its prospects. The

OK is now raced in the following countries. Austria, Australia, Barbados, Belgium, Canada, Denmark, Finland, France, Germany, Holland, Japan, Kenya, New Zealand, Norway, Poland, Portugal, Rhodesia, South Africa, Sweden, Tasmania, Thailand, USA, Zambia.

It is developing fastest in three regions: along the coast line of the northern part of western Europe; in North America and Canada and down under in Australia, New Zealand and Tasmania. It would be a very good thing if some form of regional organisation could be got together to co-ordinate action and promote the racing interests of each region.

Single handed dinghy racing seems to be increasing in popularity as more people discover the potential and the philosophy of the flexible rigged single handed racing dinghies, and it seems that quite apart from the growth that is taking place at the present time in racing dinghy classes, there is the probability that the OK will continue to attract helms men from other classes.

Some uncertainty will hang over the singlehanded dinghy until uncertainty about the Olympic singlehander is removed. It is quite possible that a future Olympic class will be a rather specialised, and perhaps expensive class and this may leave the OK to meet the needs of the large number of people who are looking for a competitive singlehanded racing craft at a moderate price. It is possible that from the ranks of these people that a proportion of Olympic aspirants will come and so that to a limited extent it might be regarded as a training class. I believe it is possible that in the not too distant future the IYRU may develop more interest then they have at moment in classes which have a training potential.

A Small Fleet in Barbados – 1967

IN BARBADOS WE NOW HAVE six OKs racing in winds that are usual pretty strong (15-25 mph) and very open water. We're all pretty good at righting the boat and the sea is always about 70°, so capsizes are almost a pleasure. We find difficulty (using Sitka Spruce) in keeping our boats up to weight. Two boats have aluminium alloy boards, which are rather an advantage – they don't warp, stick in the slot or break, and the extra weight, which isn't much is in a useful place. Expensive though. We expect two new boats to join us this year and in October the Inter-island championship (Trinidad, Barbados, Grenada) will be sailed in catamarans and OKs. We hope the other two islands will adopt the class.

Approach to IYRU for Adoption – 1964

IN THE EARLY DAYS, THE British Class Association considered the pros and cons of adoption of the OK as a British national class and had some conversations on this subject with the Royal Yachting Association. In the course of these discussions it was seen that adoption as a British national class might limit the possibilities of international co-operation and it soon became apparent that the OK in fact measured up to the IYRU yardstick for adoption as an international class in category B. With three exceptions the OK measured up to all the requirements of the IYRU.

The first exception was that the class did not control its own design, and after some negotiation with the help of the Dansk Sejlunion agreement was reached with the designer and all rights and royalties passed to the international association. The second exception was that there was no agreed international constitution or measurement rules. In the 1963 international general meeting the constitution was adopted and in the 1964 annual general meeting international measurement rules were adopted. By this time the class was ready to push for its adoption by the IYRU having secured the promise of the British RYA to sponsor the proposal, which was backed up by the Swedish, Danish and Polish national authorities.

But by this time the class policy committee of the IYRU had in fact changed their policy and the yardstick which up to now had been published in the racing rules was changed and a completely fresh set of circumstances now confronts the class. At its meeting at the Royal Thames Yacht Club, November 16-20, the Class Policy Committee of the IYRU had in front of it a number of applications for recognition as an international class, amongst them that of the OKDIA. All applications were however rejected and it was stated that in future no new classes would be accepted unless an opening had been notified by the IYRU and that in future decisions would be taken on adoption solely on the basis of trials. As however the IYRU had already declared an opening for a single handed dinghy, and they said, as the OK Dinghy has been proposed by England, it was hoped that the OK Dinghy would be entered for the single-handed trials which will take place next year. These will be organised by the British Royal Yachting Association and will be on the basis of a One-of-a-Kind event.

It is thought probable that these trials will take place in May, so that now a quite competitive element has been introduced. A design competition sponsored by the Yachting World Magazine for a single-handed dinghy has received wide publicity, and quite a number of designs have been received from various countries. The best of these will be entered in the One-of-a-Kind trials. It is thought that most of the competition that the OK Dinghy will receive will come from these recently developed boats. What matters is that we have the possibility of entering for the trial and no doubt we shall do extremely well there and no doubt it will be to the advantage of the class that it has such a widespread international distribution, and there exists so many effective national class associations as well as an international association. It could also be that the new international measurement rules of the class will facilitate its adoption. It seems that for the future it is not enough for a designer to design a good dinghy and to put it forward, it must also be accompanied by a set of measurement rules which comprehensively and effectively control the construction. The British class association will enter an OK for this event and will invite a good helmsman either from Denmark or England to take part in these trials. It is probable that a fibreglass dinghy will be entered.

A Word from Bundy – Bob Buchanan

AUGUST 1995 - AT THE Australian Championships it was my very great privilege to be awarded the Patrick Whittington Memorial Trophy. I thought it might be of some interest if I shared some reminiscences with which, in part, concern Patrick himself.

The first concerns the way in which I acquired the nickname 'Bundy'. Some years ago the NSW OK Association held its State Championships at Jervis Bay. In those days the regatta was conducted from the caravan park at Huskisson – a short stumble from the local hotel, the Husky Pub. Patrick was there – he went to most of the regattas but by this time he wasn't actively sailing, just actively socialising. A number of people were there from Victoria also.

One night (probably the first night of the regatta) we settled in pretty well at the Husky pub. After closing time we went back to the caravan park where Patrick produced a bottle of Scotch whisky. He and I sat into the small hours of the morning drinking Scotch and chatting about the major philosophical issues of the day, like whether we should go to bed or have one more drink.

The next morning I was really in the rats. Patrick was nowhere to be seen. I could hardly move, but I couldn't sleep so I decided I should go sailing. Out on the water I thought I would die. The only memory I have of the race was the conviction that at any moment I would be overtaken by a catastrophic heart attack and put out of my misery. No such luck. We went back to the beach for lunch. I couldn't eat. The most I could do was swallow a can and a half of Coca Cola which I was assured by somebody would hasten my recovery by giving me a quick glucose fix. I had to lie flat on my back on the grass. The lads oozed sympathy. Somebody said (I think Roger Blasse), "We'll have to give him a nickname – what will we call him – Scotch Bob doesn't sound right – I know, what about Bundy Bob". This concept had some perverse appeal for most of those present and the name stuck from that day to this.

In fact the first time that I ever drank Bundy and Coke was after that at Glenelg. A big front had come through much like the one that we encountered during the Nationals. Sometime during mid morning, a rescue boat was sent out to assess the situation. The report came back – the wind strength was 27 knots, at the weather mark the seas were three metres and breaking. Cheered by this substantial improvement in the prevailing conditions the OOD looked at us and said, "Perfect sailing weather, let's go."

I made it out through the breakers over the sandbar, but I was scared to death. I was too frightened to go to windward without capsizing. However, nobody seemed to notice my abject terror and in due course all necessary sound signals were given and away we went. I made it to the windward mark without any major drama and thought that I would have a little rest on the first reach. To my astonishment, people all around me didn't share my view of the lunacy of what we were doing and proceeded to plane away down the reach surfing down big waves and yelling like banshees. So I thought I should give it a go and to my surprise found it to be quite fun until – ho ho ho– the gybe mark loomed up at a great rate. Of course, in I went the moment I tried to get around the mark. But I was quickly upright and having discovered that even if I did capsize it wasn't

going to be fatal, I settled down to 'enjoy' the rest of the race.

However, good fun aside, it was cold and when we got back through the breakers, which now didn't seem nearly so terrifying, and back on the beach Bill Tyler took one look at me and said – "I think you need something to warm you up. Let's have a Bundy and Coke." So we did. Then we went back out and sailed the second race.

I was reminded by Mark Fisher (who got the story from Alistair McMichael) that the first time I went to a regatta at Glenelg I wore a crash helmet and I wore it for about a season and a half after having several painful encounters with the boom. That crash helmet was a wonderful thing – it had magical qualities – it repelled aluminium. While I wore it the boom did not touch my head once. After it rotted and fell to pieces, contact resumed from time to time though I was too wimpish to buy another one and after 10 or 11 years found that I generally didn't need it. I am now thinking of buying a set of shin pads to try and repel the traveller and keep it away from legs.

A further thought. You will all have heard the saying "Winning is not everything". This saying is used, for example, by wives and girlfriends seeking to soothe their partner's depression – "never mind dear, winning isn't everything" – in response to the news that the poor lad had just come second last in a fleet of 36 boats. I tried this on Andre when things were not going so well for either of us at the Finn Gold Cup in January. He was unmoved. Winning may not be everything but losing isn't anything.

Fast Swedes – 1972

KJELL AXEROT, THE WORLD CHAMPION, is a local lad whose rig, as one might expect, was ideally suited to local conditions. His mast and sail were the latest Marinex gear and very conventional but his boat 'Danger 6' was home built. Kjell is the student son of a rich family and sails every day with the local OK fleet. He is a pleasant lad, he bought me some beer on the last night, and very dedicated to his OK. The Swedish boats are all wood and the hull sections are dead flat with no curve in them at all and very sharp chines. The fittings are very simple and include hollow riders. Their rigs were very conventional and the sail could be adjusted to suit the conditions. Whether they used these adjustments during a race is impossible to say. The big advantage the Swedes have is experience, particularly in the sharp, choppy seas that built up so quickly at Marstrand. They hang right outside their boats with their backs upright so that they can see ahead and concentrate very hard on seeing their way through the waves.

The big thing this year is making the mast bend low down below the boom and below the deck. Masts are becoming very small at these points and [Graeme] Woodruffe's was held together with fibreglass by the end of the week. The Danes and New Zealanders had done more wood-chopping than most but the Swedes very little.

Mast and Sail – 1967

THE FASTEST BOATS ARE USING bendy rigs. This means there should be a large mast curve cut into the sail; the built-in fullness will depend on the type of cloth the sailmaker is using on your sail. Generally these sails look bigger; an illusion. It is impossible to get more cloth into the sail cutting it this way. There are three logical points to bear in mind about a mast. It should be flexible at the bottom just above the boom; this allows the whole rig to move aft when the boom is strapped down and not just the top of the mast to flex backwards, causing disastrous tightness in the leach of the sail. The middle of the mast should be relatively stiffer and this is not to make a straight section at this point but to give the mast an even bend counteracting the usual tendency for the mast to suddenly start bending at this point. Lastly the top four feet or so should whip – your thumb and index finger should easily be able to meet round this section of the mast. Sideways bending has probably had more attention than it deserves. Undoubtedly it is important to minimise it in order that the boat will point as close as possible. For this reason one can use a stiffer boom; but from the point of view of tuning a mast the fore and aft bend is the prime consideration. Lateral bend can always be cured by adding laminations later. Never be afraid to plane bits off or stick strips on to a mast until you are sure it suits you and your sail. Lightweight helmsmen are said to have problems in strong wind. This is not necessarily true! Ask yourself whether your mast really whips at the top or not. If the answer is no, take a plane to it. Masts seldom break at the top. In this way the sail shape is hardly altered, but at the aft edge the sail falls open in a gust when the boom is strapped down. This has a two-fold effect: the heeling moment of the sail is reduced particularly at the top where it has greatest leverage, and also most of that disconcerting weather helm is lost. This works every time.

OKs on England's East Coast – Jonty Sherwill

THAT FAMOUS PHOTO OF RICHARD Creagh-Osborne in OK K 111 planing into the Lymington River must have inspired many to try the OK Dinghy in the early 1960s. On the East Coast of England several fleets soon got going including on the River Deben at Woodbridge (Deben Yacht Cub), Waldringfield and Felixstowe Ferry Sailing Clubs.

Situated just five miles apart Waldringfield Sailing Club and 'The Ferry' provided a perfect contrast of sheltered but tricky up-river racing or full-on open sea action in big seas and strong tides at the river entrance. Competitive racing was already well established with leading lights including Bob Garnham in the International Sharpie class and Jack Knights, three times British Finn champion and reserve helm for the 1956 Melbourne Olympics.

Simon Bullimore is credited as having the first OK Dinghy on the Deben at Waldringfield in 1964 but was soon followed by Jem Goddard who swapped his old Fairey Finn for an exquisite OK K 642 built by Harry Poole. In this pale yellow 'Flook Too' he would be almost unbeatable, setting the highest standard of sailing and boat preparation to inspire a thriving local fleet.

In 1970 the British Open Championship was awarded to Felixstowe Ferry and attracted not just British entries but from Europe too. In a week of wind and waves Denmark's Steen Kjølhede dominated the fleet in a beautiful varnished boat. Steen used a new style Hamlet sail as did Richard Wilde who was crowned British National Champion. Both he and the runner up Jem Goddard were sailing all-GRP boats by local builder Seamark Nunn, Goddard using a locally made Seahorse sail that had already won the 1967 Nationals for Mike Richardson.

The group photo of competitors and helpers (all championships should do this) includes several individuals who made major contributions not only to OK sailing at Felixstowe Ferry but also to running the wonderful Deben Week annual family sailing regatta where hard racing, hard drinking students could win prize money to support their lifestyle.

Deben Week no longer happens but an enduring memory is of seeing future 505 World Champion Peter White borrow an orange Henriksen OK to win the Clarke Cup trophy race on the final day in 1971. The boat belonged to Paul Andersen, a Danish employee at Seahorse Sails who later sold it to Ferry OK pundit Stan Sawyer, who for unknown reason named it 'Powerful Pussy', quite typical of boat names of that era including 'Hoof Hearted' and 'Poppy Tupper'.

Boosted by the Ferry championship the standard of local sailing continued to rise but the emphasis was always on having fun as anyone who experienced a Saturday night at the Ferry might conceivably remember. Daniel Dahon (F 437 in photo) summed it up at that British Open Championship in 1970: "We drink and we p**s, we drink and we p**s!"

Sailing the five miles between Waldringfield and Felixstowe was relatively easy with a fair breeze, while travelling by road was only slightly further but occasionally seemed to be a lot harder. Rapid post-race rehydration at the Ferry bar or the Waldringfield's Maybush Inn was no doubt a contributory factor in some fabled incidents.

One describes a convoy of cars with boats on roofrack or trailer heading through the lanes to the Ferry at above usual speed. A gentleman in a new Triumph Herald stopped unexpectedly and an OK landed on his roof. Clearly he was outnumbered and told that the whole incident and

From Top left clockwise:
Felpham 1979, James Bridge
Butler and Don O-Donnell
with 'Fury';
Harwich Nationals 1975;
Waldringfield Easter 1974

any damage caused was completely his own fault.

Another is of an OK Dinghy sailor who lived halfway between the two clubs and lost control of his mother's van on a sharp bend. The vehicle leapt into a field of maize, fully-grown and ripe for harvest. With zero visibility the driver kept going in a bid to rejoin the road but flattened most of the crop in the process. After repairs, that old van soldiered on until finally meeting its end in collision with a row of parked cars in South London.

Despite other minor setbacks like these east coast sailors maintained regular appearances on the World Qualifier circuit, while back at Waldringfield a competitive junior programme provided a regular supply of new talent for the OK class. Two of these younger sailors appeared to treat their OKs as disposables, being cheaper to replace than repair. Thankfully they reformed and are now mainstays of both the OK and Finn classes. The name? Deaves!

Crucial to the success of the class in the early days was the supply of locally built competitive wooden boats by Dick Larkman and Mike Nunn, while in the mid 1970s John Cook at Harwich Town deserves credit for producing low cost but fast stitch 'n' glue plywood boats but with a twist – glass fibre tape on the inside only. The technology may be very different but today Synergy Marine and Idol Composites are maintaining this east coast legacy.

With British Championship success over the years for local sailors

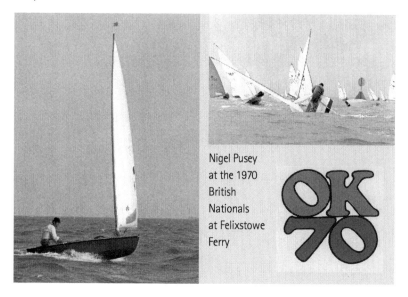

Nigel Pusey at the 1970 British Nationals at Felixstowe Ferry

including Mike Richardson in 1967, Jonty Sherwill in 1978, David Rose in 1988 and 1990, Dave Carroll in 1997, and Robert Deaves in 2006 and 2013, in 2017 it was local legend Tim O'Leary who flew the east coast flag by heading to Barbados for the 60th anniversary World Championship, a fitting reward for three decades of devotion to the OK class as competitor and measurer.

The author of this piece has just refitted a 1970 all-varnished wooden OK Dinghy that first raced at Felixstowe that year. Built by Millican & Shipsides in Lancashire this eye-catching boat was owned for 45 years James Bridge-Butler, British OK Class chairman from 1974 to 1977.

Laid Back Leith – Bob Ross

Reproduced from Australian Sailing 1990.

QUIETLY-SPOKEN NEW ZEALANDER LEITH ARMIT, who on Port Phillip Bay this summer for the third time won the OK Dinghy world championship, prepared for the worlds on that most unlikely of training grounds – the upper waters of Sydney Harbour.

And Armit, who has been living in Sydney for the past year, has been a strong influence in the revival of the singlehanded international class on Sydney Harbour.

The new energy has come from the Drummoyne 16ft Skiff Club on Birkenhead Point where Peter Horne got the OKs going by rounding up second-hand boats and encouraging some former OK sailors to dust off their boats.

Armit, a boatbuilder, who spent nine months in Sydney four years ago, building an 18ft skiff for Rob Brown, said: 'When I first got back here, around February last year, I came down to Drummoyne and saw the OKs racing. Peter Horne loaned me a boat to go out sailing with the guys and eventually sold it to me for what he had bought it for.'

"Since then, the fleet has increased in size and the guys are a lot keener. They have bought new sails, masts and boats and I am sure they will hold that enthusiasm even though the worlds have just been held in Australia and a drop-off in interest could be expected."

There are 15 or so OKs sailing from Drummoyne. They combine with OKs from Mosman Amateur SC, a traditional stronghold of the class, to race down harbour on Saturday afternoon and off Drummoyne on Sundays.

OKs are being built in Sydney again, by Guy Phillips of Woodtech Boats, Glebe. Local sailmaker Marc Sier has developed, with the help of Armit, a sail which Armit says is a good all-rounder. And masts are available from Goldspar. To put a new OK in the water from these suppliers would cost, Armit estimates, less than $5000

With good local gear available, he sees the Sydney fleet as again challenging the supremacy of the Melbourne OK sailors who have been predominant in the class recently. "Several young guys are keen to get into the class and buy boats," says Armit.

"I think the fleet will build up to 25 to 30. I will still help the class as much as I can with information and helping set up new boats and hopefully get the competition up here going strong and challenging the Melbourne domination."

Armit's knowledge of OKs and feel for the boat is profound. He is 29, has been sailing them since he was 16 in Auckland. In his second season, he finished second in a world championship, in Holland. He won the worlds at Torquay, England, in 1983 and at Medemblik, Holland, in 1985. He has had spells away from the class – campaigning for Olympic selection in Finns in 1984 and 1988 an sailing aboard Canterbury Export in the New Zealand Admiral's Cup team of 1985.

Armit's preparation in Sydney was quite different and more pleasant than for his earlier campaigns from Auckland. Instead of towing the boat down to Takapuna for racing and long sessions straight-lining on open waters, he would drive to Drummoyne, pull his boat out of the

rack (the OKs are stored in the club for free!) and down to the water.

He raced both Saturdays and Sundays and Tuesday nights as well, against seven or eight OKs in the Birkenhead Point Marina twilight fun race. "The conditions here were a little different to what I had been used to with boat traffic, tide, many more obstacles but I found it more interesting in a way. And having this club backing the OKs is a tremendous asset to the class."

"Instead of just going separate ways after racing or training, here you come in off the water to a social scene where you can discuss in comfort the sailing and learn from each other's experiences. That sort of thing makes the training so much more enjoyable and I appreciated it very much after lonelier years in New Zealand."

Most of Armit's physical preparation came from "time in the boat". He did do some gymnasium work early in the season but then cut it out because he felt he was becoming too heavy. Then he caught bronchitis and lost a lot of weight. "Since then, I have just been doing a little bit of running to keep fit and try to keep my weight down." He sailed at 83 kg in Melbourne.

Armit planned his campaign so that he went back to New Zealand with enough time for some sailing before the selection trials to check his speed. He made some changes to his sails after the NZ trials and then used the Australian championship and the period before the worlds, to finally sort out his rig.

He started the season with a Bellair (Terry Bellair, Melbourne) sail and with Sier developed a similar sail. "We put a bit more shaping into it, especially in the bottom to improve downwind speed and to make it a little bit easier to sail with – not as sensitive to sheeting."

"Being fairly consistent in making the sails enabled us to make quite good gains – if we made an alteration, we could see what it did."

"Marc was a great help. I was very happy with the sail we developed which I used in the nationals (finishing second to Australia's Mark Fisher) and had good speed, especially in fresh breeze and moderate airs.

"I decided to try another sail in the week between the nationals and the worlds, partly because I did not want to alter the proven sail and to try for possibly a little more light-air speed. It was a matter of matching the luff round to the mast."

Armit eventually used that Paul Page sail on a Needlespar red top mast. He used the Icebreaker hull he had built himself in 1983 from the Gary Lock owned mould. "This is a class where you can build boats strong enough to last through a good period of racing and still be very competitive," Armit said. "They are built out of foam/sandwich; fibreglass and Divinycell or Klegecell. You are not allowed to use exotics."

Armit, third after the first four races with 3-5-8-4 placings behind defending champion Per Hagglund of Sweden (7-13-1-1) and Fisher (4-3-3-9), won the last three races to win the championship with a loss of 23.7 points from Hagglund 42.7 and Fisher 46.1.

Armit explained that because of big and unpredictable temperature-influenced wind swings on the world championship course at Black Rock YC, he had decided against taking too many chances in the early races but as the series went on, he sailed less conservatively. "Once I had some numbers on the board. I sailed a little harder, knowing I could afford to have a drop race and my chances were improving. We had some light races and others with a bit of breeze that sorted out the whole fleet. The last three races were all tough."

In the last race, Armit set out to be somewhere near Hagglund around the first mark after a conservative beat, in the 18 knot breeze, confident that he was faster on the reaches than Hagglund. "I went from fifth spot to first on the first reach and even more ground between us on the second leg for a comfortable lead.

Why was he faster on reaches? "It's in the technique of sailing the waves, being comfortable in your boat and knowing how far you can push it," says Armit.

Winning a world championship for the third time drew a typical comment of the modest Armit: "I was pretty pleased about the whole thing."

He is now looking at a campaign in Finns towards the next Olympics possibly as an Australian if it possible to become a citizen in time.

Meantime, he will continue to support the OKs at Drummoyne with such advice to newcomers as: "The class can take a fairly good range of body weights – anything from 10.5 stone to 14 stone – by adjusting the rig to suit your body weight."

"You can do a lot developing rigs for your body weight and get to learn a lot about how a rig works, so the OK is definitely a training class for the Finn as it was designed for."

Mast rake! "It depends on the cut of the sail. You cannot put a figure on it; a lot of it is on feel. You can put down starting points for tuning but from there it's feel."

"Set up the rake to sail with the end of the boom on the deck, or close to the deck, especially in a breeze. I sometimes sail with it fractionally off the deck so if I want to get a bit more height, I can pull it down an inch more and get it. Most times it is pretty much on the deck unless I want a bit more twist. A lot of guys just tend to sheet in harder as the breeze goes up when they might be sheeting too hard and it may pay to ease off a little bit. I keep telling them you have to play around with the mainsheet tension just to get the leech working."

"Upwind, you have to steer an OK and use your body weight to get through and around the waves. The controls have to be constantly changed as the conditions change – Cunningham, outhaul, inhaul – and the traveller line should be in the hand all the time, worked with the mainsheet to control how much twist you want in the sail.

"Technique has a lot to do with sailing an OK. You don't need to be super fit. Upper body strength is not as important as in a Finn. It is mainly a matter of getting out there and conditioning your legs for sailing. And I have done that this season, just by sailing. It's generally the best way; just time on the water, sailing."

New Rules for International Status – Jeremy Firth

FROM THE OKDIA NEWSLETTER 1972 – Now that negotiations with the IYRU over international status are nearing completion it is fitting to give some account of the work of the ad hoc international technical committee.

This committee was set up by the annual general meeting of OKDIA held in Marstrand in August 1972. Its brief was specifically to co-ordinate the revision of the measurement rules with special reference to the suggestions and comments of the IYRU. The committee composes Jeremy Firth (Australia) chairman, Franck Ducourneau (France), Steen Kjølhede (Denmark), and Ian Miller (Great Britain).

The committee met several times during the Marstrand Worlds and considered the written suggestions made by Alf Lock, chief measurer at the Auckland Worlds two years earlier. Unfortunately the comments provided by French officials from the 69 series were not available in a satisfactory English translation at that time.

On basis of these considerations, extensive consultations have been undertaken with IYRU Measurer Tony Watts. Most of the detailed work has been done by Ian Miller who fortuitously belongs to the same yacht club as Tony Watts. Jean Smith has been acting as secretary to the committee and the OK class has yet another reason to be grateful for her untiring co-operation.

The new rules, the current draft of which has now been circulated to National secretaries, have intentionally been modified only to clarify existing interpretations. Efforts have been made not to introduce too serious changes to existing building practices. For example it has been clear for some time that an additional measurement is required to control keel spring between station 3 and the two existing stern measurements (Nos. 27 and 28 on the current measurement form). However to introduce this rule immediately so that all new boats have to conform (from say 1st March 1973, when the IYRU finally accepts the OK) is grossly unfair to any manufacturer with a glassfibre hull mould that does not conform. The committee proposes that warning be given of the new

rule so that it can be introduced in November 1973 or November 1974 when the IYRU normally reviews the rules of all international classes.

Other areas where the old rules have been clarified include:

1. Administrative sections which have been modified to conform with standard IYRU procedures.

2. All sails will need a manufacturers serial number.

3. Side-deck assembly has been clarified.

4 Hull curvature – both longitudinally and transversely – is now controlled.

5. Chine radius – the wording of the 15 mm radius rule has been clarified.

6. Centreboard – the method of measurement has been modified to place more measurement emphasis on the profile of that part of the centreboard actually protruding below the keel.

7. The distance of the rudder from the transom has been limited.

8. The mast and boom measurements have been revised to prevent extreme wing masts, over-rotation, and asymmetric bearing rings

9. Sail measurement wording has been modified to conform with standard IYRU practice.

10. A towing eye near the stern is now compulsory equipment.

The current state of play is that the wording of the rules (that replace the 'red form') are nearly complete. Tony Watts is currently producing a draft of the measurement form (replacing the 'black form') and a set of measurement drawings. The IYRU will be responsible for redrawing the plans so that some of the detail on them conforms more closely to current practice. The basic plans and profiles will obviously remain identical with the existing OK plans.

Once the IYRU and OKDIA agree to all these changes – and to the new OKDIA constitution (formerly the 'green form') – the OK will have gained status as an IYRU international class. From the formal acceptance date (which could be March 1973) all new OKs must conform to the new rules to gain measurement certificates. OKs with valid measurement certificates dated before the IYRU acceptance date but which do not conform to the IYRU rules will have a further two years in which they may sail in IYRU administered competitions without modification. After the two year 'period of grace' they may no longer be eligible for these competitions. A period of grace for National Events would have to be negotiated with the countries' own National Authority.

In conclusion, it is necessary to add a disclaimer. This report was written by the undersigned and does not necessarily represent the combined or personal views of the ad hoc Technical Committee members (partly because of the obvious communication problems). But hopefully it will give a more or less accurate statement of the current (26th January 1973) position.

The OK Dinghy in South Florida – Fritz Mueller

DETAILS OF THE OK DINGHY'S true origins are sometimes disputed, however there will never be any doubt that there has always been a strong Danish-American connection. Consensus has it that the collaboration in the late 1950s between Knud Olsen in Denmark and Axel Damgaard Olsen in Seattle produced the original drawings and prototype, and ultimately launched the class in North America. The real oddity in this story is the birth of an intensely competitive fleet of OKs racing at the geographical antipode of that hollowed ground, Seattle.

In the early 1960s, and beyond the nucleus of the class established in Seattle, the OK Dinghy class had already achieved reasonable success and distribution throughout the United States – quite an achievement considering the distances involved. By 1964, there were about 650 boats registered nationally – with the largest concentration of fleets in the Pacific Northwest, and Southern California. There were other active fleets formed in the USA's midwest, which benefited greatly from occasional participation from a very strong Canadian contingent based in Ontario.

It was in the second half of the decade, that OK Dinghy racing got its start in the idyllic Biscayne Bay area of South Florida. There, it flourished until the mid-seventies. In Florida, the earliest small groups of OK Dinghy sailors were spread around the northern half of the state, and were chiefly influenced by the California fleets. The earliest sailors were concentrated on the upper west coast near Clearwater, with another small group of boats active in the West Palm Beach area, on Florida's east coast. Interest in the class rapidly moved southward toward Miami, which was already recognised as a centre for world-class yacht racing. As early as 1968, there were about 20 boats seriously racing in the greater Miami area. Among South Florida's early pioneers in the class were Fred Bremen, Bill Blood, Ted Long, Emory Kamps, Paul Lindenberg, and Rick Grajirena.

Most of the early hulls in South Florida were either home built or brought in from the west coast of the USA. Paul Lindenberg, of West Palm Beach, built a mold, and eventually became the local builder of

glass boats. By mid 1968, he had completed six boats. They were beautifully constructed with Baltek balsa core, were extremely fair, and had
state-of-the-art glasswork. Moreover, they were fast, and rapidly over-
took the demand for Clark-built hulls coming from the Pacific Northwest. As interest grew in the area, more and more sailors started building
their own boats – the Coyner brothers (Wayne and Doug) built theirs
according to conventional techniques, while the Ostlund brothers (Stel-
land and Goran) opted for the composite technique using fiberglass taped
seams, a relatively new method at the time which was becoming popular
in Europe. Spars were most often either home built, or built by Bill Blood.
A National Airlines pilot and captain, Bill was somewhat of a visionary
who carved out quite a reputation for lightning fast Optimists made from
aircraft grade materials and construction methods – Sitka spruce, super-
light plywoods and epoxy resins – with a minimum of fastenings. His OK
Dinghy spars were works of art, and technologically highly advanced. Sail
design was rapidly being developed by Fred Bremen of Bremen Sails in
Miami, and at Levison Sails in Clearwater, Florida.

Racing interest in the class took off rapidly, and was fuelled by
keen competition amongst the locals, many of whom already had
significant racing experience on an international level – Rick Grajirena, Gary Carlin, Ding Schoonmaker, Fred Bremen Jr., and Sennett Duttenhoffer were the ones to beat. For almost a decade, the
OK Dinghy was perhaps the most competitive racing class on Biscayne Bay, except for the Star Class or Snipe. For many of the local
'Rock Stars', the OK Dinghy was a second boat, something in which
to hone singlehanded dinghy and tuning skills, and a venue providing an opportunity to compete against those who were already well
recognised in other international classes. The extreme level of local
competition also drew many younger sailors to the OK Dinghy, and
most came directly from the well-established Optimist and Sunfish
class junior programmes in Miami.

The class was well organised at the local level, and several of the top
sailors travelled to participate in nationally organised events or those
such as CORK in Kingston, Ontario. One year, the group returned from
racing in Canada at CORK, dumbfounded by Ib Andersson's blazing
downwind speed in drifting conditions…sailing backwards. The fleet had
a local newsletter, called 'Telltales', published once a month. Bi-monthly
'meetings', i.e. parties, were the norm.

The fleet founders embraced all newcomers, and there was a remarkable sense of fraternity, competition and sportsmanship for all. Many

racing sailors will acknowledge that since the Olympics in 1968, the sport of yacht racing went into world-wide period of transition – in virtually all classes. For the South Florida OK Dinghy sailors in the 1960s, it was still a time of no real weight carrying limits, sailing by the rules, and no professionalism. In those days it was not unusual to see the OK Dinghy tyros coming up from junior programmes, attempting bravado and wearing 20 kg of wet sweaters, courageously sailing their OKs with stiff wooden masts…all the time emulating such Finn greats as Carl Van Dyne, Jorg Bruder, and Willy Kuhweide.

Boats and equipment evolved in Florida over several years, and by 1974 the fastest hulls were Lindenberg (W. Palm Beach), and Kjølhede (Denmark). Technology originating from the Finn Class was always to have a dominant impact on speed developments and was immediately transferable to the OK Dinghy.

Bruder spars, imported infrequently from Brazil, were coveted. A few sailors even used the then-new delaminating masts that he developed originally for the Finn, and which were adapted for the OK Dinghy. In general, spars built by Bill Blood, and some home built, were still quite competitive. The best sailmaker was Bremen who developed a unique luff rope system for distributing tension according to chord length, and who had a very special talent for matching mast and sail combinations for the OK Dinghy…in the days of wooden spars, this was really and art form difficult to duplicate.

The South Florida fleet was fortunate to achieve several milestones in its relatively brief period of existence. The Bremen Challenge Cup, intended as a World Team Racing Championship, was started in 1969 by Fred Bremen Sr. and was open to registered fleets worldwide. For the first few years, this trophy exchanged hands several times between the South Florida and Barbados fleets. The last known winner was the Alamitos Bay fleet from California, sometime during the early seventies. It could be a real benefit to the class if this trophy could be resurrected, with a possibility of including a short team racing series in conjunction with the World Championship.

In 1970, the South Florida fleet began hosting what is called in the United States a 'Mid-Winters', actually, something of a winter National Championship. An annual event which had tremendous success (considering geographics), it often drew as many as 40 boats from all over North America. Past winners were Chris Boome from California, Rick Grajirena, Fred Bremen Jr, Sennett Duttenhoffer in 1973, and Fritz Mueller in 1974.

In 1971 the South Florida fleet inaugurated its most prestigious award, the Ted Long memorial trophy, to honour the fleet champion. A beautiful OK Dinghy half-model, it memorialised the local Englishman and pioneer of the class who died tragically of a heart attack while at the helm of his OK Dinghy during the US National Championships on Lake Erie, Ohio that year. Joe Kolisch was the last to win that distinctive honour in 1975.

The United States sent a small team to the World Championship in Falmouth in 1973, made up entirely of South Florida sailors: Joe Kolisch, Glenn Carlin, Tom Stocks, and Fritz Mueller. It will always be remembered as a real blowout, with winds consistently in the 20-35 knot range, huge seas, and a two-hour trip to the starting line. There was never a light air race, not even a medium breeze. Clive Roberts from New Zealand showed everyone how it was done under those extreme conditions, and won convincingly. The US contingent was somewhat hindered by inexperience, borrowed equipment, and breakdowns. None the less, the team had a wonderful time, learned tremendously from the international competition, and forged many friendships that continue to this day.

By 1975, the South Florida fleet was beginning to feel the same pressure that all other OK Dinghy fleets were feeling worldwide – the popularity of the Laser. The Laser's simplicity, with a strong network of dealers, made it the boat of choice for those who were looking for a singlehanded sailing dinghy – right out of the box. The writing was on the wall for the South Florida OK Dinghy fleets, and eventually as newcomers became scarce to the OK Dinghy, most sailors moved onto other popular dinghies such as the Lightning, Snipe, Finn, and Laser.

Racing An OK Dinghy In Waves (Big Ones) – Axel Olsen

THE FOLLOWING MATERIAL (1965) WAS picked up from Axel Olsen who seems to know as much as anyone about the subject. He was kind enough to grant this interview some time ago.

"I hate waves. I enjoy sailing in flat water in a good wind. The worst wave actions you can have are the unpredictable ones without a pattern like waves left over from a dying wind or backwash from bulkheads or bridges. For this type of thing I have no good answer. For the purpose of this discussion I will talk about normal wave conditions with the waves increasing according to the strength of the wind.

Upwind – If you are racing in good wind with little wave action, move your weight forward and sheet your traveller close to the centreline of the boat. When wind and waves increase you move your weight aft and move traveller outboard. The reason for this is when the waves are higher the angle of attack has to be greater so you have more drive to go through the waves. The weight is moved aft to keep the boat as dry as possible. (Less water aboard, less weight to carry.) If the nose is too low in the water you get a large spray which ends up in the cockpit.

When racing in big waves, point higher between waves and when close to the breaker, bear off and try to cut through it. You sail a zigzag course. The worst problem in big waves is in tacking. Try to get maximum speed and tack where you can find the greatest distance between big waves or in shallow waves. Push the tiller hard to throw the boat over fast. If you don't succeed in your turn you are sold out because the waves will push your boat back and you will fall in irons. If you are in irons, push the tiller to leeward until the boat starts to fall off. Get up speed and try tacking again.

Downwind – This is the only time you get help from the waves. When running downwind, if the wind is strong enough to start you planing, you use the waves to start planing. You watch the waves coming and when you are about to go over the crest, pump your sail (careful to be legal) to increase your speed and get on the down hill side of the wave and pick up enough speed to start planing. Try to ride on the downhill side of the wave as long as you can. When you hit the next wave on the uphill side, you steer a higher course and then repeat the process.

Reaching – In reaching parallel to the waves if the centreboard is all of the way down the force of the waves may trip you. Raise the centreboard about half way so you can side slip some but still steer a course.

Jibing – Jibe when the speed is the greatest if you have the guts. You have less hull resistance when you are planing and there is less pressure on the sails when the boat is at maximum speed. So jibe then.

General – Never pull the centreboard up all the way. Have it rigged so it will hold its position. Then, if you capsize, you can use the centreboard as a lever to right it. Have the hatches well secured and watertight. Make sure the mast has a pin so it will not float out if you capsize. Wear a lifejacket. Tie a knot at the end of the mainsheet so it won't get away from you. I also tie the end of the mainsheet to my belt so that the boat won't blow away from me if I capsize.

The Wind is King – Bill Tyler (and Jan Tyler)

The Corona King of Wind event was a one-off invitation event in Makung, now Magong, in the Penghu Islands of Taiwan. OKDIA was approached during 2002 to join the 49er fleet in 2003, which had already taken part in a previous event. The whole event was sponsored by the Taiwan Tourism Bureau to develop the island's tourism industry. Boats were flown out, yes flown out, on China Airlines, and were ready and waiting by the quayside as the sailors arrived. Three sailors came from the UK, one from Australia, one from Belgium and one from New Zealand to join a handful of local sailors for whom boats were send out from the UK. It was an epic undertaking for six 30-45 minute races. Bill Tyler takes up the story.

THE SAILING EVENT WAS A bit of a 'Mickey Mouse' affair, much as expected, purely a marketing tool to promote the sponsors' products. Having said that, the organisers did a good job trying to keep everyone happy as things got difficult later in the week.

The main problem was that the north-easterly monsoon arrived a week or so earlier than expected and blew away the event after only the first few days. This was unfortunate as the major sponsors, Corona Extra and Land Rover, had their gala days scheduled for later in the week on Friday, Saturday and Sunday. All of the on-shore activities went ahead as planned but there were no sailing events for the people to watch other than a few keen wind-surfers. Needless to say, the organisers had to work hard to keep their sponsors happy, so the non-sailing sailors were left to sort things out for themselves over the last few days.

Thanks to the generous sponsorship arrangements from Corona Extra and the organisation of the guys from DMI (Destination Marketing International), US$5000 prize money was allocated to the OKs for the event. Land Rover provided a number of their vehicles for the use of the organisers and competitors. This allowed all who wished to do so to tour the three main islands which are linked by bridges to form a horse-shoe shape 'inland sea' location for the sailing area. Maggie and all of her helpers from the Taiwan Tourism Bureau worked tirelessly throughout the week to ensure that all visitors were made to feel welcome at the event. Other sponsors, China Airlines and Uni Air, provided discount travel arrangements whilst HBO and MTV provided media and entertainment support.

After a good flight we arrived in Taipei, sorted ourselves out and met a few more of our group, then found our way via shuttle bus to organised overnight accommodation at the CKS Airport Hotel.

The trip from the hotel the next morning for our flight to the Penghu Islands was expected to take about an hour in the morning peak-hour traffic. The timing was too early for the hotel shuttle bus back to the International airport to link up with the International airport/Domestic airport service, so mini-bus transport was arranged the night before. This was a disaster but nevertheless quite amusing in hindsight. The guy with the mini-bus arrived late and couldn't fit the ten of us in with all of the luggage. He obviously didn't want to lose the job so he phoned home and arranged for his wife to come on down in the family car to take some of the guys. Seemed like a good idea but she didn't have a clue as to where she was going. Fortunately, Jan and I were in the bus with others and the luggage so we missed out on the drama. Our driver was constantly on the phone giving directions to his wife as we were driving to the airport. We had to stop and wait at one stage as he raced up and down the road trying to find his wife to get her back on track. At one stage she apparently nearly wiped them all out as she changed direc-

tion under phone instructions across three lanes of traffic to make a hard left turn to leave the freeway. Eventually she got the other guys to the airport and we all raced to the check-in around 0715 to try to get on our scheduled 0740 flight. None of us had tickets at that stage and only one guy had any idea of the arrangements – and of course, he was in the car. After a lot of hassle we all got on the plane, which was delayed for us and we eventually left Taipei around 0800. The flight to the Penghu Islands only took about 40 minutes – full plane, 56 passengers.

We were met at Makung Airport by Barry, one of the DMI (Destination Marketing International) staff and he organised us all in two taxis and one of the sponsor's Land Rovers to drive to our accommodation at the

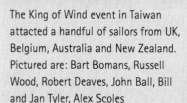

The King of Wind event in Taiwan attacted a handful of sailors from UK, Belgium, Australia and New Zealand. Pictured are: Bart Bomans, Russell Wood, Robert Deaves, John Ball, Bill and Jan Tyler, Alex Scoles

Penghu Youth Activity Centre. The welcoming committee were there with media cameras recording the proceedings as Louis, the boss of DMI, introduced himself to us all and took charge of booking us into the 'Resort Hotel'. We were in room 412, not too bad – good view over the entrance to the boat harbour and beyond, and looking west towards the Kuanyin Pavilion. Good, very clean room and polished floors with sleeping facilities consisting of mattresses on the floor and a tiled westernised bathroom, much to Jan's relief.

We unpacked and settled in, then went for a walk along the foreshore to the 'Sailboat Hall', as it is known, only about five minutes or so from the hotel, where we attended to necessary registration etc. It was hot with very little breeze at that time and many of the boats, mine included, had not arrived as expected, so no practice sailing that day.

We went back to the hotel for a rest and relaxation in the air-conditioned room before getting ready for the Opening Ceremony from 1900 on. This was a major event, out in the open forecourt near the sailboat hall where a huge MTV stage had been set up with full disco light-and-sound equipment equal to anything you would see at a rock concert. The opening act was an eastern drums performance with adults and kids taking it in turns to show us their skills. You can imagine the scene (a little goes a long way) and this seemed to go on forever. Then there were speeches from the VIPs, the local dignitaries and the sponsors before the sailors were invited up on stage to be introduced on mass to the large audience of locals. This was followed by the closing act consisting of a local dance group performing folk dancing in their traditional costumes. Before and after the formal activities, the disco music blasted away with the professional DJ controlling the stage. All very impressive and very, very, loud. We then had an organised local BBQ, which was not so impressive and consumed some of the major sponsor's free Corona beer.

After a good night's sleep on our hard mattresses on the polished floor, we were up and about at 0800 to learn of our buffet breakfast arrangements for the week. This was served daily in a large dining room area on floor 2 of the hotel. A good time for a chat with other sailors; OK and 49er guys with a few partners. The day was again hot and sunny with a light to moderate breeze building throughout the day. The boats had arrived overnight as expected after being delayed in Taipei for a few days, which caused a bit of a panic for the organisers.

We unpacked the boats and found everything to be OK except for a minor indentation on the bottom of my boat which was easily covered by a small piece of gaffer tape, so of no real concern. Rigged the boat and then off sailing for two races on the day. The 49ers sailed a different course arrangement and had four races on the day.

From our 11 entries we only managed to get 9 OKs out on the water. Our fleet was not very strong as the only top guy to come was Bart Bomans from Belgium, our current European Champion. Russell Wood from New Zealand was our next best and the OKDIA Secretary, Robert Deaves from England, was third overall. The next four, including me, were of similar standard and the rest of the guys and girls were only newcomers to the OKs, sailing borrowed boats to make up the numbers. Nevertheless we were there and hopefully some future benefit will be gained for the OKs in the Asia/Pacific region. After the sailing, we had another BBQ for dinner, again not too good, together with more of our major sponsors' free Corona beer.

The next day was again hot but the wind had freshened to 15-18 knots. We had another two races and I finished 5th in both. I managed to beat the local Taiwan guy, Pan, who was a good strong bloke around 30 or so who had a lot of Laser experience but had never sailed an OK before. Still couldn't beat the fourth placed Pom, John Ball. The 49ers again sailed four races on the day.

In the evening there were no special organised activities other than the MTV, so eight of us from the OK group went downtown to a local restaurant in the fishing harbour area where we had a beautiful meal of traditional dishes with fish and crustaceans, etc. selected live from the tanks on the street front outside of the restaurant. Another great evening with a few drinks, just for a change local Taiwan beer. After dinner we strolled around town a bit and then found a handy bar where we had a few more beers before heading off home for the night.

Again, usual start to the day and again, hot and sunny. Wind was very fresh early and showing signs of getting even fresher. After breakfast, five of us had a turn with one of the sponsors' Land Rovers, so we set off on a tour of the local area. The Poms were in charge with John the driver and Robert the navigator. Russell, Jan and I tagged along for the ride. While we were on the unprotected windward side of the island and looking out over the Taiwan Strait, the wind was really starting to blow very hard and we had trouble keeping our balance. I made an executive decision and decided there and then that I would not be sailing that day.

As soon as we arrived back at the club, Jan and I set out to explore the town together and we had a great day walking up and down all of the narrow streets in the old section of Makung before returning to the club to see what was going on. The 49ers had shown good judgement and had decided to stay on shore but unfortunately a few of the OKs chose to sail so they completed two more races on the day. As it turned out that was the end of the sailing.

During the evening the wind continued to howl and the MTV played on. We watched a rollerblading and skate-boarding exhibition before missing out on most of the pizza which was the supplied evening meal. No free Corona from the sponsor on the night and the party turned into a fizzer. Some people were not happy, John in particular. He had broken his boat during the afternoon's racing and then when he couldn't get some free beer it all proved to be a bit too much.

He had a point but there wasn't too much that the organisers could do about it on the night if the sponsors decided to turn the free beer off. Anyway, as a matter of principle, we were not going to pay for our 'free' Coronas so we decided to get out of the wind and took off on mass down to a local Karaoke Bar. The guys and girls from the Canary Islands were the leaders of the push on this one and the OK group tagged along for the night. We had a good laugh and also a few more Taiwan beers.

More of the same the next day, breakfast as usual, weather, sunny, hot and howling wind. The wind had continued throughout the night. Most of the sponsors' tents and shelters had blown away and the boat park looked a pretty sorry sight. Our OK area was in the less sheltered part of the boat park so we had the remains of the Land Rover tents wrapped around our masts and boats. Bart and Audrey, the Belgians, had woken up at 0400 and went down to the boat park to check on our boats. Bart had to clear away some of the mess from our boats then and we all moved the OKs later in the morning to a more protected area around the corner of the boat park area. Fortunately no damage to any boats so again we were lucky.

Needless to say, no sailing today for anyone other than the windsurfers and only a few of those guys braved the conditions. The 49er guys rigged one boat with a smaller rig and tried to have a 'speed trial' event but they couldn't keep the boat upright and eventually broke some gear. All a bit of a nonsense really as by this time it was blowing about 40 knots.

Dinner was down at the sailboat hall. This was a very good feed as the local people, we presume from the tourist group or sailing club members maybe, put on a great dinner of traditional dishes with everything you could possibly imagine. There was plenty of variety and the dishes just kept coming so everyone was able to take their time and enjoy the meal in a nice quiet dignified way instead of the usual rush of the previous nights BBQs. John's displeasure the night before must have achieved the desired result as the sponsor's free Corona beer was back on for the night. Another good night had by all.

More of the same next day yet again. Still blowing and no chance of sailing. An attempt to organise some team sports games during the morning failed, so it didn't really happen. We sat around and talked until the usual lunch arrived as it did on time every day. A packaged mix of a few small dishes, maybe meat, chicken, rice, vegetables, etc. Chinese style. All OK and most of it you could eat. After lunch we packed up the boats and generally started to get ready to go home as the sailing had just fizzled out.

We got cleaned up and went back down to the club for the closing ceremony. The wind was still howling and the MTV was still blasting so it was not quite as pleasant as the opening ceremony. However the brass band played on to open up the proceedings, followed by the speeches and the prizegiving. Fortunately they restricted this to the first three placegetters in the 49ers and the OKs so it did not go on forever. They had originally intended to call up every competitor one at a time to introduce us all to the crowd but this would have been hopeless given the windy conditions. After this we had Taiwan's answer to Kylie Minogue and her rock band and all the local kids doing what kids do at pop concerts, gathering around the stage and jumping up and down during the performance. All very impressive but thankfully we were able to drift away as we had to attend the Corona official farewell dinner at our hotel. This could have been great as they set it up in the open courtyard which was reasonably protected from the wind. The free Corona beer started to flow but the BBQ again was not very good. The night continued on a downward slide after that. The Corona girls and the dancing girls put on a bit of a show, then the VIPs departed and the free Corona beer dried up. We all sat around for a while wondering what to do. Will we go downtown or not? Some did and some didn't.

The next morning we packed up the boats and said farewell to those leaving the island on the day.

Overall, this was a pretty hectic but mostly enjoyable event. Definitely a different experience, some negatives but much more positives and well worth the effort. It was a great opportunity for the OKs to be seen at a new venue with extensive media coverage. Hopefully we will be invited back again. *ED – we were not.*

From the 1965 OKDIA AGM Minutes

A selection of items from 1965.

• THE SECRETARY commented on the growth of the class during the past year, particularly in Sweden and Britain, where there was a combined increase of approximately 500 a year. New countries to introduce the OK include Finland, Japan and Thailand. There had been surprisingly few problems in the application of the new rules. The new drawings had been prepared and these had resulted mainly from the work of the technical committee at Roskilde last year

• ON THE proposal of the OK Comite Nederland the world championship series should be sailed with one mast and one sail only, except of force majeure. A lengthy discussion resulted in the defeat of the proposal, there being 25 votes for and 33 against

• A PROPOSAL by ASPRYOK that the entries for the world championship series should in future be limited to 80 boats was discussed at length by the meeting. Svend Jakobsen remarked that experience both at Roskilde and Hayling indicated fair racing resulted from fleets of 100 or 120 boats. James Ware and Roger Morgan (BOKDCA) also spoke against the proposal which was eventually defeated by 31 votes for and 35 against.

• SVEND JAKOBSEN proposed that races should be started on the beat, and secondly that the chairman of the race committee of a world championship should always be someone who knows all about the OK. The general feeling of the meeting was that this might produce difficulties, as this particular individual may not always know the water and may not have the local knowledge of the man of the spot. There must be no disagreement between the club arranging the world championship and OKDIA. The secretary thought it a very good idea if the committee formulated some ideas for running the championship; these could be put in front of the club puting on the event.

• PATRICK POULIGNY of France asked whether fibreglass masts are now allowed. Sweden and Britain expressed their interest and both countries offered to test such a mast if one could be made available to them.

The Pilot Remains on Board – Thorsten Schmidt

IT WAS 60 YEARS AGO that Knud Olsen drew the OK Dinghy in 1957. The International OK Dinghy community is celebrating this anniversary throughout the year 2017, but the German OK story is not quite so long.

In the beginning, this new, challenging singlehanded sailing dinghy spread mainly in the Scandinavian countries. The triumphal procession through the two German states began with a few years delay. In the West, two germ cells soon established themselves: in Hamburg, you had to jump into the OK Dinghy when you were young and wanted to be part of the unadjusted long-haired rock stars of sailing in the middle of the 1960s. But a fleet at the TSVS also quickly developed in Kiel.

One of the first German OK Dinghy sailors was Norbert Petrausch, whom we all call only Peit. As early as 1965, he sailed with GER 39, a self-built boat, on the Kieler Förde. Already in the following year Peit and his friends from the local scene built 12 brand new OK Dinghies in one batch (one was his GER 46) on a farm near Kiel. Although there were initially difficulties in getting the new boats out of the mold, the release agent used did not work, but after a few attempts, water pressure was able to pop the hulls out of the mold, if not, then the flanges were torn off.

In 1968, the first OK Dinghy built by a shipyard, a Danish Henriksen, bore the number GER 101 and was made entirely of plastic and was the coolest stuff money could buy. Even today one can admire this boat and its sailor in action. In the TSVS, a large-format photograph (in black and white, of course) with GER 101 in the middle is certainly worth a look into the OK past and Peit at a young age.

In the following days, new OK Dinghies followed each other: GER 218 and 243 in 1971, then the GER 330, an OK Dinghy from the Scharping shipyard in Wedel/Hamburg in 1973. Of course it helped that his parents' house was only 300 metres from the new Olympic centre in Kiel-Schilksee, but there was simply nothing more important for Norbert than to sail OK Dinghy. In 1980, he bought again a brand new Henriksen OK GER 563. Peit finally acquired the Hein OK GER 630 'Pitty-Platsch' in the unmistakable colour design, with which he has sailed since 1986 to the present day.

As early as 1983, Norbert Petrausch was elected as the second chairman of the German OK Dinghy Class Association. From 1990 to 2017, he was the chairman of the class. During this time, Peit organised many international OK Dinghy events, arranged for perfect German cham-

pionships of our class, took care of the regatta calendar, OK info and all the annoying stuff associated with a registered club in Germany.

Our class has literally benefited from Peit's good connections to practically all important people in sailing in Germany for decades. Everyone knows and appreciates Norbert, he has prevented our class from being deleted from the Kiel Week programme, organised after short-term cancellations of regatta organisers and has been taking over the organisation and the race direction of our Whitsun-Regatta for years as a one-man team.

It is therefore no wonder that he was admitted to the OKDIA Hall of Fame as early as 2008 at the world championship in Warnemünde, and is acknowledged on an international level.

The class did well under its leadership, the OK Dinghy scene is showing great international growth, many new buildings and newcomers also show in Germany, against the general trend in many other classes, the unbroken attractiveness of the OK Dinghies and are an indication of Norbert's good work.

In 2017 Norbert Petrausch retired as chairman and was made honorary chairman of the OK-KV. The fact that he cannot retire but is an important part of our community is already the gift of the OK sailors. Now, Peit can sail the regattas with a brand new sail and the personal sailing number GER 1.

Even in stormy times for sailing, we do not need to worry about the OK class. The pilot remains on board – thank you Peit.

Weight Concentration –1966

FROM CORRESPONDENCE WITH MEMBERS OF the International Technical Committee, we have learned that in one or two instances, OK Dinghies have been built, in which some solid timber components have had their sections substantially increased to provide a weight advantage. Although this involves problems of definition, there is no doubt that this practice is in conflict with Measurement Rule 1, paragraph 1, and measurers having boats presented to them for measurement in which this form of advantage has been obtained, must report this avoidance to Rule 3 (13) under Item 80 of the Measurement Form.

The purpose of this letter is to suggest that you ask each entrant to the World Championship at Veere, 6th-12th August, to make sure that his boat meets Measurement Rule 3 (13), read in conjunction with Rule 1 (1). Boats presented for measurement at the World Championship will be carefully examined in respect of this rule at Veere and those thought by the Measurement Committee not to measure in this respect, will not be permitted to sail.

During the World Championship, the Committee will carefully consider what action, if any, should be taken with regard to clarification, definition, or addition, to Rule 3 (13).

Mediterranean Revival – Henri Bérenger

IN THE SUMMER OF 2013, after a rather boozy lunch at the home of my friend, Daniel Dahon, one of the top French OK Dinghy sailors, Daniel takes me to the bottom of his garden and shows me an overturned hull which must have been there for several years: it was an OK Dinghy.

The traces of time showed, a bee's nest - a real one - a hole in the deck at the bow…

Daniel says, "Do you want to take it and refit her?

Silence.

Going through my mind are memories from a distant youth. Was it the effect of the good wine?

"OK, I'll take it."

Under my terrace, in Sanary, I set up an unlikely 'workshop'. This was towards the middle of July. There followed lots of cleaning, scrubbing, sanding, repairing, painting….

One month later I was loading the dinghy onto my trailer, and heading for Les Sablettes. I was ready for the launch. It was the very same day as Daniel Dahon's birthday.

At around the same time, not too far away, Jean Louis Petetin, President of the Sanary Sailing Club, also inherited an OK Dinghy built between 1965 and 1970. This one belonged to the father of his friend Michel Bonnefoy. It had a hull made of polyester and a beautifully renovated varnished wooden deck.

So here we are in Les Sablettes, Jean Louis and I for the traditional 15th August Regatta, also called the Two Brothers Regatta ….what a symbol.

With old sails, a wooden mast for Jean Louis, an old Needlespar for me, it was such a pleasure to be once again at the tiller of an OK Dinghy in my hand after so many years. It felt as if we had never stopped sailing OKs, despite being a bit out of practice at the helm and with the tuning.

A promising revival began while sailing in Sanary Bay, much to the surprise of young and old onlookers

"Isn't that an OK Dinghy?"

"What sort of boat is that?"

We capsized for the first time, but the general impression was very encouraging.

Jean Louis, who is particularly enthusiastic, starts to campaign for his new passion and goes surfing on the net, finding countless useful addresses which show that the OK Dinghy is not a thing of the past, but on the contrary, it is very popular, particularly with our Northern European friends, who have apparently not given up on it as we have done for decades.

Contact is established at ASPRYOK (French national association of OK Dinghy owners), with its President, Frédéric Lamarque, who put us in touch with 40 or 50 French nationals who sail and take part in regattas all over France.

The idea is taking shape in our minds. What about organising a gathering of OK Dinghies in Sanary?

Joining us were Yan Rialland (Toulouse), Patrice Rovere (Paris), Didier Soulier (Lacanau), Patrick Debaere (Lacanau), Maxime Fraggi (Lyon) and Bernard Coursières (Montpellier).

Some locals came to enhance the group of Southerners: Laurent Petetin, Xavier Beckius and also Jean Pierre Gailes from Cannes, who was one of most famous French OK sailors in the sixties and who had just bought and refitted an OK, increasing his fleet of Finns and Dragons.

We had a memorable return to our youth, despite windy mistral conditions, which didn't stop the most intrepid sailors in the group. There was a great atmosphere both in the port and at sea.

At sea, Daniel has put on his coaching outfit.

In port, the Société Nautique de Sanary welcomed everyone in its traditional fashion, with its aperitifs and snacks, which are much appreciated by both the OK sailors and other folk who have come to savour the atmosphere in Sanary.

It was an unmissable occasion to tell and listen to good old OK Dinghy stories.

This small gathering met again in August on Lacanau Lake where 30 OKs participated in the Sud National Championship.

For the Bandol/Sanary team, consisting of four sailors who made the trip, it was an opportunity to evaluate the level of OK Dinghies in France and to enjoy a hospitable welcome at Lacanau.

It is the beginning of much speculating: aluminium masts, carbon masts, wooden masts....North sails...

The winter of 2014/2015 gave the Mediterranean Yolists time to improve their equipment and to recruit new talent. Gérard Bonnet (Bandol) bought two OKs which he refitted. Tim Petetin, Jean Louis's worthy son, acquired one, which also needed to be repaired.

When the 2015 season opened, we met up once more in Sanary, for some hotly contested races and some unintended swims.

The Lacanau National Championship followed in August with a team of four Yolists from Bandol and Sanary, headed by Gérard Bonnet.

Back in Sanary again, in October there were three days of regatta in autumn weather. A new local Yolist joined in, Jean Christophe Morin, from the Yacht Club des Sablettes, sailing in Gérard Bonnet's second OK.

2016 was the Carbon Year.

A spirit of rivalry descends on the group of Yolists as to who can fit out their boats the best. Thanks to some of Daniel Dahon's international

Above: Daniel Dahon
Below: 1969 World Championship at Bendor, an island off Bandol

contacts, Laurent and I each inherit a new carbon mast, which comes almost directly from…Auckland.

The newly acquired North sails, allowed us to boost the performance of the team and we looked forward to great results in the forthcoming regattas.

In May 2016, in Bandol we sail together with the Finn series, a beautiful regatta in light wind: good conditions for Tim Petetin to confirm his pretentions, and for Jean Christophe Morin to try out one of Gérard's Yoles again.

Shortly afterwards, Fabien Capellières turns up with a beautiful OK Dinghy (Icebreaker), straight from England, which is the newest boat in our fleet, along with Jean Pierre Gailes' one. All this is bound to give ideas to certain people…

In August 2016 we are back at Lacanau: Jean Louis, Laurent, Tim, Gérard and myself, having just returned from Quiberon where the OK Dinghy World Championships was held. Bernard Coursières and I were the only two Mediterranean sailors. Jean Pierre Gailes came as well, but could not sail due to health issues.

We won't dwell on the ranking…but what a wonderful week of true regattas, with very good wind conditions, very high level competitors and more than 100 on the starting line.

In Lacanau, we had got used to light winds … this edition has been the worst.

The 2016 season ended with a beautiful weekend in Bandol, with some Mistral and fine weather, as is often the case, and confirmation of a fleet with younger competitors and newer equipment: Jean Pierre Arrighi, Tim Petetin and his brother Pierre, and also Gilles Bérenger. Family stories.

Jean Louis christened his new British boat (Idol) OK, purchased in Belgium … where the Belgian national championship was held in Antwerp.

A few days later, Jean Christophe Morin raised the level of the equipment once again through his purchase of a recent OK model (Vejle).

ED - The revival continues with more new boats and sailors and this growth prompted the class to hold its 2018 European Championship in Bandol.

From Langweer to Oosterzee – Wietze Huitema

SOMEWHERE AROUND 2010 I RAN into the De Vries family from Oosterzee at a regatta weekend in the town of Langweer. Looking for a sailboat to get back into sailing just for fun, and searching the internet, my eyes spotted an OK Dinghy. chined, unstayed mast, nice history.

While restoring an old OK Dinghy that I found, I noticed there was this regatta with two OK Dinghies on the starting line. Addie Tange sailed NED 305, formerly sailed by three times Dutch OK Dinghy champion Piet Verstelle. The other OK Dinghy, NED 555 was sailed by Jan Siebe de Vries from Oosterzee. After the races I went up to these two sailors to get acquainted. Jan Siebe's parents Harm and Ingrid, were also there and we got along quite well.

At that time little did we know about the history of the OK Dinghy sailing that went on in the second half of the 1970s and early years in the 1980s. Langweer was a special place for OK Dinghy sailors. First of all it was the hometown of another three-time Dutch OK Dinghy champion Ids Bakker. It also was the hometown of the young Hoekstra brothers Hessel and Sipke, two brothers that are back on the Dutch OK scene over the last couple of years. In the 1970s OK Dinghy sailors from other parts of the Netherlands got together for training on the lake and came ashore for lunch with soup at the Bakker family house. Not Hessel and Sipke, they went home to 'us mem' (Frisian for mother). The other sailors were Hans Hoedeman, who also won the Dutch OK Dinghy title three times and became Ids' brother-in-law, Herbert van der Veen and a young man with the surname of Velema. Both Ids and Hans also did a lot for the class association in their time. The house is still there and the walls are filled with pictures from the Dutch OK Dinghy history. I know because I had the privilege to meet Mrs Bakker a couple of years ago to obtain an aluminium mast. She enjoyed telling me about the old days.

The fact that the family de Vries and I met some 40 years later in this town would start of the rebirth of the Dutch class and more importantly it was the spark that would lead to the new international regatta for OK Dinghies in Oosterzee, named the Eastersee Regatta. Contact was continued through email and meeting each other at races where Jan Siebe participated with his OK Dinghy. We promoted the boat at the Watersportsfair Boot Holland where some people believed the OK Dinghy in the Netherlands was dead. We professionalised the Dutch OK Dinghy sailing website and sailors started to meet each other at national and international regattas like the Spring Cup and the Belgian nationals. Jan Siebe raced the Europeans in Medemblik in 2010 with an all-wooden rig. A lot has changed since then in the Dutch class.

In 2013 the idea was born to have a sailing event for OK Dinghies on the lake Tjeukemeer near Oosterzee, the hometown of the family de Vries. We thought we would start with just a day and invite sailors to come over and sail at the lake together. Ronny Poelman from Belgium brought his boat and along with him six or seven OKs went on the water. They liked the location and the idea for a real (inter)national OK Dinghy regatta at Oosterzee was born. The next year Ronny promoted the first edition of the Eastersee (Frisian for Oosterzee) Regatta at the famous café Brakeboer during the Spring Cup.

By the end of August 2014 we had nineteen sailors attend the first edition of our regatta. Frank Strelow was a great winner but most of all we had a lot of promoters for the 2015 edition. We settled for the last weekend of August to have a fixed spot on the international sailing calendar. In 2015 the number of entries raised to 37. Again Frank was the winner of the regatta so back-to-back wins for him. Unfortunately not sailing but as a spectator at the regatta we met with Hessel Hoekstra who was planning a come back to the class after 40 years.

In 2016, bridging a 20-year gap the Eastersee Regatta was the official Dutch OK Dinghy class championship. And Hessel and his brother Sipke returned in their OKs. It was great to have them; experienced sailors but great men as well. And they had lots of stories from the past, talking about their hometown Langweer and the weekends they sailed the lake with their friends. Dirk Dame became the Dutch champion in a fleet of 42. Hessel and Sipke battled each other to end on spots 14 and 15 just like years before.

Jörg Rademacher won the 2017 edition of our regatta, but unfortunately was not the new Dutch champion due to lack of races. With 48 sailors from Germany, Poland, Belgium, Luxemburg, Great Britain, France and of course the Netherlands, the event is growing each year and we hope to remain on the calendar for the next couple of years. We hope the Hoekstra Brothers will sail with us till they are grey and old. And perhaps in 40 years time people will have memories about sailing their OK Dinghies in Oosterzee just like we are talking about the memories from men sailing their OK Dinghies in Langweer today.

Finally World Champion – Thorsten Schmidt

KARSTEN HITZ BEGAN TO SAIL the OK Dinghy at the early age of 13 or 14 years old. Under the watchful and critical eyes of his father, Rudi, the boy, who at that time was much too skinny, made his rounds on Lake Segeberg (between Hamburg and Kiel) and fought with the too large sail area and the capricious qualities of the dinghy.

With his buddy Sven Wurmdobler, Karsten sailed every weekend, not only learning to master the boat but also to sail really fast. So Karsten, who lived right on the lake, spent his youth sailing, and soon nothing was more important in his life.

His father drove Karsten to the first races and accompanied him during the regatta weekends. Although Rudi was generous in dealing with other sailors and really having fun for everyone, he was strict and relentless to Karsten.

Karsten sailed his first world championship in 1978 in Medemblik, The Netherlands and two years later in 1980 in Varberg, Sweden he became junior world champion. In the following decades Karsten not only dominated the German OK Dinghy scene, winning many German championship titles, but also dominated in the major European regattas. He repeatedly won the international regattas in Medemblik, Kiel and Warnemünde, was Danish champion and in his cupboard collected OKDIA ties, won through his many top ten finishes at the world championships.

Karsten was often the favourite to win in the run-up to a world championship. But just as often he failed in the title fights for different reasons. The highlight of his personal tragedy was the injury at the 1999 World Championships in Neustadt, Germany. As the outstanding sailor of the season Karsten was the top favourite for the title and but had injured himself while waterskiing before the championship. A thigh injury prevented his participation and what was considered to be a sure victory.

No wonder that winning the world championship became a kind of obsession for him.

In 2000, the world championship took place in Leba, Poland. Again Karsten was favoured, but another sailor was also obsessed with thinking about becoming world champion. Nick Craig had arrived in the top league of the OK Dinghy class during the previous year and wanted to end the 'English curse' after so many years: Never before had a sailor from Great Britain won the world championship in the OK Dinghy.

The weather conditions during the world championship were in Karsten's favour. A lot of wind and high waves on the Baltic Sea on the first three days ensured that Karsten led the series comfortably with a 1-5-1-1 score with outstanding downwind speed. But on the fourth day of the regatta the wind took a break. There were short steep waves from the days before on the race area and Karsten finished in 15th place. Would the big favourite from Germany now lose his nerve with the unloved light wind conditions?

The second race of the day took place in similar conditions with little

wind and unpleasant waves, but Karsten showed his skills in the style of a champion and won with a start to finish victory.

Karsten had four wins in six races and only one race was planned for the final day. What at first glance seemed like a comfortable position, was, on a closer look at the list a really threatening constellation for Karsten. Nick Craig, the big challenger from England, had been able to win a race but otherwise had sailed a flawless series. And Nick had the better discard with fourth place as his worst position.

Nick can count and of course he saw his chance on the eve of the final. If he were to be two places better in the last race than Karsten or if the German would come in worse than sixth place, the Englishman would be world champion.

What was Nick planning to do?

Already the day before Karsten learned about the plans of the Englishman. Bart Bomans, who finished third in the series from Belgium, had no chance for the title. By chance, however, he heard a loud conversation in the shower between two Englishmen. Nick announced that he wanted to sail the German back in the last race by a kind of match race to be world champion.

Karsten found out about the English match plan over beer in the evening. In real OK style, he drank another one or two Polish beers that night, ensuring a deep, restful sleep.

In moderate wind conditions on the last day the stage was prepared for the big showdown. Already 20 minutes before the start Nick approached the leader and tried to impress Karsten by aggressive manoeuvres and psycho-games. And indeed, just a few seconds after the start sequence, he announced a first protest against Karsten. With much shouting and aggression Nick pursued his opponent right through the waiting field of the 80 OK Dinghies. Although Karsten was forewarned, he still seemed surprised by the vehemence and determination of the challenger. At the pin end Nick was able to manoeuvre the German and himself over the line too early.

The start attempt ended in a total recall and the duel before the next start went on.

Like the apocalyptic riders, the two leaders ploughed through the field again. Nick felt disabled several times and suspected team sailing from some German OK Dinghy sailors.

With the distance of the years one can say that we other German OK sailors were of course on Karsten's side, wished him well, but there was not even the thought of helping him by team sailing. Most German OK Dinghy sailors, even if they wanted it, would not have been able to sail in this manner.

I, myself, trusted in Karsten's sailing skills and actually tried to prevent him getting drunk the night before.

Karsten had meanwhile grasped the seriousness of the situation and utilised his outstanding boat handling. The German managed to escape by a clever manoeuvre a few seconds before the start of the pursuit and managed to start perfectly. Nick was trapped by other boats (not Germans) and was slow to pick up the pursuit from the third row. In this last race Karsten finished second just behind the great Dane, Jørgen Lindhardtsen, unaffected by Nick Craig, who finished only 14th.

The Englishman did not give up even now. Nick Craig submitted four protests to the race committee, but all were rejected by the jury and Karsten was finally world champion of the OK Dinghy 25 years after his beginnings on Lake Segeberg.

In the following year Karsten defended his title in Båstad, Sweden, again superior and was for the second time and this time undisputed OK Dinghy world champion.

Friends Knew no Mercy – Peter Scheuerl

IN THE LATE 1980S AT Kiel Week, the event lasted one week with only one race a day, sailed right in front of the marina.

It was a very sunny and warm day with no wind and everybody was bored. Luckily at that time some of the grass areas in front of the buildings were not covered with party or shop tents. Some Australians had the stupid idea to announce a rugby challenge, and several others were even more stupid to accept it. Later when I went to the first aid people for a possible broken toe, they just said,§ "another one of the rugby players?"

But we made the biggest local newspaper with the headline "and then the friends knew no mercy", as there was no sailing to report on that day.

Carbon Fibre Masts – by Don Andrews

Don Andrews was Chairman of the OKDIA Technical Committee from 1998 to 2001. This was written in 1994. It would be another eight years before carbon masts were brought into Class Rules.

1994 – SINCE THE LAST OKDIA annual general meeting, at which the technical committee was asked to keep the question of carbon fibre masts under review, there have been two important developments. First, at an informal meeting of European members at the European Championship in Neustadt in August 1994, a request was made to the technical committee to bring a proposed rule change to the 1995 AGM which, if approved by both OKDlA and the IYRU, would bring carbon fibre masts within our rules on 1 March 1996. This was reported in the secretary's newsletter in September 1994. Second, the German OK Association has asked for permission to experiment with carbon fibre masts and this has been granted by the officers of OKDIA subject to ratification by the 1995 AGM. This permission is available to any national association but can only be brought into operation during racing if the approval of the national authority of the country in which the racing takes place has been obtained. The permitted use of carbon fibre masts must also be written into the notice of race and sailing instructions for each regatta.

Clive Roberts Wins 1972 Interdominions – Bill Tyler

EXTRACT FROM BILL TYLER'S CHRONICLE – Seventh Interdominion Championship was held in New Plymouth, NZ at the New Plymouth YC, Easter 1972. Won by Clive Roberts, New Zealand from John Douglas, New Zealand 2nd and Wayne Watkins, New Zealand, 3rd. This was definitely a 'big boys' contest. Winds of 25-35 knots whipped confusing seas on top of four metre ocean swells to create sea conditions described as making Somers look like a 'Sunday school picnic on a fish pond'. There were plenty of swims but fortunately little gear damage considering the conditions. Clive gave a magnificent exhibition of heavy weather sailing to win the seven races of the series for a perfect score. Sailing borrowed boats from the 1970 Worlds Brian Collins, Vic. placed 11th, Bill Tyler, NSW, 19th, Bill Bell, Vic, 22nd, Graeme Walliker, NSW, 23rd and Val Gersbach, NSW, 27th. This event really was something special. The seas had to be seen to be believed. You would scream down the face of one wave only to then stop in the trough and look up to the crest of the next one to see other OKs floating almost an entire mast height above you. I had never sailed an OK in conditions like these before and still have not sailed in anything similar since. On shore the hospitality of the Kiwis was fantastic. A once in a lifetime event – truly a great experience.

OKDIA Constitution – Don Andrews

THE NEW CONSTITUTION WAS, AS expected, accepted by AGM in February 1986. Without going into fine detail, it works something like this.

First, the members. These are the National Associations with 30 or more members, and since they range from Great Britain to New Zealand and include a very diverse group of nations, it is not at all any easy task to keep the members in communication with each other. Associations with less than 30 members can become associate members, with limited powers.

Second, the function. Klaus Wigger, OKDIA secretary and treasurer, wrote more fully in a previous Newsletter (Autumn 1985) but the main responsibilities of the international association are to maintain the one-design, to encourage the development of the class, and to arrange international events.

To achieve these objectives, OKDIA has three major policy making and decision making bodies. The first is the technical and rules committee, with a chairman and an unspecified number of members. Its job is to advise on class rules and their interpretation. The chairman is an ex officio member of OKDIA Committee.

The second is OKDIA Committee, with a president, two vice presidents, one each for the two hemispheres, a secretary, a treasurer – functions which may be combined – and up to four other members. Its job is one of general management of the Association's affairs. In order to ensure that all members have the opportunity to contribute to the work of the Committee arrangements are made for a good deal of written communication through the secretariat

The third is the Annual General Meeting. This is constituted to ensure that all member associations are represented in accordance with their size, the small associations with 30 members or less having one vote – There is some confusion about this in the constitution. Clarification is being sought – 30 to 100 two, and over 100 three. Again, arrangements are made for postal communication and proxy voting.

This constitution certainly tries hard to make a difficult situation workable, but no matter how carefully the structures are thought out, not much will happen unless the individual member associations and their committees put some time and effort into making things happen.

Real Sailors Only – Peter Scheuerl

AT ONE WARNEMÜNDER WOCHE IN the early 2000s, it was very windy and the race committee had posted long postponements. But as it is common with some classes, the Lasers and Pirats (German two person boat) had blocked the ramp ready to go. Soon after the race committee decided that only boats for 'real sailors' should go out as only they could handle the conditions. So a loudspeaker announcement was made, "Can the Lasers and Pirats please vacate the ramps, so the OKs can go sailing."

Memories of an OK Friend – Bill Tyler

RICHARD PATRICK PITCAIRN WHITTINGTON WAS born in India on 4 August, 1942. He was the second of three sons of his British parents and was educated in England where he attended University and graduated with an Economics degree

Patrick first came to Australia from England in early 1971. Shortly after settling in Sydney he purchased his first OK 'Jo Jo', KA 306, and joined Mosman Amateur Sailing Club. I met Patrick later that year when I too bought my first OK 'Rhubarb', KA 220, and also joined the club at Mosman. During that first year sailing and socialising together, friendships were made that were to last over many years. Old OK Dinghy names such as David Treglown, Chas Yates, Val Gersbach and Geoff Comfort were amongst Patrick's closest friends in that first year's sailing and their encouragement saw him journey to Mackay in North Queensland for his first National Championship. The stories that were told of 'Lizard Hollow', the camping area where the OK competitors and their followers stayed at Mackay, were enough to convince me that OK Nationals were a 'must-do' from then on.

A few months later over Easter 1972, the NSW Association sent me to New Zealand to compete in my first Inter-Dominion Championship at New Plymouth. The great time I had there only reinforced my allegiance to the OK fleet – but that's another story. At the same time those who stayed at home travelled to Griffith NSW to contest the inaugural Easter Riverina Championships. This event was to become a bi-annual fixture on the NSW programme over the next few years coinciding with the New Zealand Inter-Dominions as an alternate contest for those who could not make the trans-Tasman trip. The Griffith regatta became the 'yardstick' for social OK events much the same as Horsham is in Victoria to this day.

Patrick attended this first Griffith series along with 36 other keen and thirsty OK Dinghy sailors. 'Newswok' July 1972 records details of this event including a paragraph on the running of the 'Champagne Stakes', a race which was sailed in high winds on the Saturday night starting at 11.00 pm. The article states that 12 boats took to the water in pitch-dark and light rain and that all safety precautions were observed. Patrick was awarded a special prize for this race as 'Best Vocalist' having completed the course singing extracts of Handel's Messiah. Even in this, his first full year of OK sailing, Patrick was demonstrating his philosophy for participation in OK events. Total enjoyment through the whole range of activities from sailing to socialising was a basic fundamental of this philosophy.

The National Championships at Holdfast Bay, Adelaide SA, in 1972/73 introduced us all to David and Zita Coleman. Shortly after that event, David and Zita returned to Sydney from Adelaide to live and joined us at Mosman Amateur Sailing Club. Over the years that followed, Patrick was to adopt the Colemans and the Tylers as his Sydney based OK families and he always knew that he could find a bed or a sympathetic shoulder in time of need at either of our family homes. At this time too, Patrick also adopted Val and Dawn Gersbach as his country family and for many years after he spent much time staying in Wellington enjoying the hospitality provided by the Gersbach family. In those early years also, Patrick was to share his Mosman household with another old Mosman OK identity, Ted Curtis. Patrick and Ted reminded us all very much of 'the odd couple' – Ted with his tidy domestic habits and Patrick – well, enough said.

In 1973/74 we returned to Holdfast Bay for the Nationals and the world championships that followed. These events saw Patrick's sailing philosophy extend to the International arena for the first time. Torben Andrup and Jørgen Lindhardtsen, the two Danes who finished first and second in the worlds that year, visited Sydney after the event and stayed with Patrick and Ted. Indeed Torben, the most laid-back world champion we are ever likely to meet, had such an enjoyable time that he stayed on for many months and became very much a part of the local OK Dinghy scene.

Through the mid 1970s, Patrick played a very important part in the control of the NSW OK Dinghy Association. Firstly as Treasurer and then as Secretary he assisted Rod Laing-Peach, Howard Taylor and myself with the necessary administration of our association. On the sailing front, we progressed through the years of dominance of Bill Bell and then Bruce Ashton as we competed at national championships in Brisbane, Melbourne, Sydney, Hobart and then back to Adelaide once again. No matter where we sailed, Patrick was there to participate fully in all sailing and social activities. On the racecourse he would usually finish up towards the tail of the fleet, but finish he did on the majority of occasions in fair winds and heavy weather. On shore in the social events, Patrick was a clear winner outlasting all who issued a serious challenge. His renditions of such well known songs as 'Rule Britannia', 'Jerusalem' and 'We Were Sailing Along on Mosman Bay', as well as countless other lesser known British college and football songs, will long live in the memory of those who knew him well. Visits to Morso in Denmark to view the 1976 Worlds and to Auckland in New Zealand for the 1977 Worlds, allowed Patrick to continue to develop his International reputation as an OK Dinghy legend.

In 1979 Patrick decided to return to England to pursue further career goals. As he wasn't in too much of a hurry, he managed to fit in a cruise to San Francisco via Fiji and a visit to the Rockies before meeting up with Peter Gale in Amsterdam en route to Tonsberg in Norway for the world championship. Patrick was appointed unofficial Team Meister for the 'Down Under' teams, helping Terry Bellair and Peter Gale to overcome minor problems and handling on-shore matters for the Kiwis including the eventual winner of the event, Rick Dodson. To quote from Patrick's report on the event: 'One of the features of the series was that the team manager had to go to all social functions free and even to a special one only for team meisters with an OK moored in the swimming pool. To me the ultimate was being asked by the President of the Swedish OK Dinghy Association to have my photo taken with him. I tried to point out Doddy but he was not interested in a mere world champ'. This instant success in the newly found career as a team meister was to spur Patrick on to even greater achievements.

Once he was settled back in England, Patrick went back to college to obtain additional qualifications to allow him to commence teaching and college lecturing. He bought a cottage in which to live at Westbourne in West Sussex and once again joined the work force. He also purchased another OK Dinghy, K 1790, with the intention of continuing his sailing activities. For one reason or another, mainly cold and wet weather, his racing campaign didn't quite live up to the high standards he had achieved back 'home' in Australia.

The European summer of 1981 saw the OK Dinghy worlds held at Hyères, France with a very good Australian team of six competitors which included youngsters Mark Fisher and Peter Jackson and one unofficial team meister. I don't know that Patrick contributed much to Peter Gale's on the water success, but nevertheless his record as a team meister stood at two out of two at the completion of the event. Following the worlds, Peter Gale and Peter Jackson visited Patrick back in England. Reports indicate that it was a very heavy week with bad weather and lots of socialising and the infamous Scimitar under the tractor incident. Fortunately no injuries – to quote from Patrick's letter to me shortly after the accident – 'Minor accident which looks much worse than it was as I was only doing about 5mph when we hit. The car being fibreglass collapsed rather easily onto Chocko's head which is his least sensitive part.' Needless to say, both Peters made it back to Australia in good condition leaving Patrick to cope with yet another English winter even though he would have much rather returned with them to the wonderful land of Oz.

Patrick sailed K 1790 in the 1983 British Open Nationals at Torquay, England as a warm-up series for the worlds. This event was won by Glen Collings, with Alistair McMichael sailing K 1970 second overall and winning the British national championship for the second time. As Alistair has since also won two Australian championships, this is something of a unique record I would think. Although Patrick's boat number was similar to Alistair's, unfortunately his on-the-water performance wasn't and he finished 90th in the fleet of 98 boats

This was a good omen for the teams from 'Down Under' as Patrick was not required for the British team and he was able to again take up his unofficial position of team meister for the Australian and New Zealand competitors. It was at this series that a very young and inexperienced Andre Blasse made his OK Dinghy world championship debut. Again to quote Patrick – 'Andre (Renee) Blasse was a bit outclassed but is a very nice lad.' Things certainly have changed over the years – Andre is still a very nice lad although now older and wiser but he does not get outclassed in world championship company any more.

At the conclusion of the 1983 Worlds, Patrick's teams had performed exceptionally well once again. Leith Armit won the first of his world championships with five of the top ten places being filled by members of the 'Down Under' team. On the social scene, Patrick's prodigies performed with considerable merit with some reported quotes – 'perhaps the highlight was the indoor games evening, with victory going to the Australians.' 'Nobody on the boat trip will forget in a hurry Jacko's Aussie sing-song', and, 'Where did Jacko sing for his supper? – at the Devonian.'

It seems Chocko had a birthday during the series and he obviously did his best to live up to Patrick's high standards for all-round series enjoyment. On the water however Chocko managed to upset the jury, to again quote Patrick, 'Unfortunately he was disqualified for pumping – I thought it very dubious as the weather was heavy and told Klaus so.' To finish off what must have been a memorable fortnight, Patrick won a Tiga sailboard as first prize in the raffle and his record as a team meister now stood at three out of three.

A few months later in September 1983, Patrick returned to live in Australia and took up where he had left off in 1979. OK Dinghy sailing in Australia was at that time, as usual, dominated by the Victorians with Glen Collings winning three nationals in a row. During his reign as champion, Glen successfully fought off the challenge of the established contenders such as Mark Fisher, Peter Takle, Bruce Ashton, Terry Bellair and others, as well as the challenge from a bunch of newcomers to our class as they quickly developed their OK Dinghy sailing skills. Chocko and Andre were joined by younger brothers Mark and Roger and others including a youthful Peter Milne, Phil Dubbin, Wayne Andrew and of course the unforgettable Neil Williamson. All of the above also displayed much potential with their social skills and that talent was quickly spotted by our experienced team meister. Patrick soon adopted all of this lot as his collective Victorian family and he contributed a great deal of time and effort in assisting them to realise their outstanding potential over the next few years.

The 1984-85 Australian Championships were hosted by the NSW Association at Toronto, Lake Macquarie in December, 1984. This series is best remembered by those who attended for the indoor games events so hilariously organised and controlled by Patrick along similar lines to the games held in England during the 1983 Worlds. Patrick's newly acquired Victorian family performed with distinction both on and off the water demonstrating that they too had quickly learned all of the important principles of the Patrick Whittington philosophy for participation in OK Dinghy events. What is not as well remembered is the fact that the Toronto Nationals would not have happened without the necessary organisational skills of Patrick and Howard Taylor who together made all of the arrangements for the event.

Patrick returned to Europe once again in 1985 and met up with members of the 'Down Under' OK Dinghy teams for their assault on the Dutch open and the worlds at Medemblik in Holland. The Australian group included the by then experienced Mark Fisher and four of Patrick's young Victorian family – Roger Blasse, Neil Williamson, Mark Jackson and Peter Milne. If ever there was a job for a team meister this was it. The stories of this trip vary depending on whom you talk to, but needless to say all of our intrepid youngsters gained much valuable experience from their participation in these events. Just the fact that Patrick was there to lend his support must have provided sufficient inspiration to the experienced guys from 'Down Under' as they filled the first three places in the Dutch nationals – Mark Fisher, Leith Armit and Nigel Soper in that order – and then further success in the worlds with Leith winning his second title, Mark a creditable third placing and Nigel finishing overall in tenth position. Roger, Neil and Mark Jackson all had good results in the worlds, but Peter didn't have much luck on the water in Medemblik due to unspecified physical ailments which apparently required much attention from the local medical people including many sessions with a certain female physiotherapist.

After the worlds in Holland, Patrick and four of his team journeyed to Ishoj in Denmark for the Open Nordic Championships where they enjoyed the Danish hospitality and performed well in all the onshore social activities. Peter obviously had responded well to his treatment from the physiotherapist in Holland as he was able to participate with much enthusiasm in all activities whilst in Denmark. So much so that he was recruited as third member of the Danish team for the Teams Trophy event at the British Nationals which were held soon after the completion of the contest at Ishoj. The team photo of the Danish team at that event which they won features two tall blonde Danes and one mischievous grinning dwarf in the middle looking just like a troll from Scandinavian folklore. At the completion of this European campaign, Patrick's record as a team meister stood at four out of four.

By the end of September 1985, Patrick was once again back in Australia looking forward to the coming season's events – the 1986 Nationals in Melbourne and the 1986 Auckland, New Zealand worlds. My memory is vague regarding OK Dinghy sailing happenings around that time. I know that Mark Fisher won both of the events but I did not go to either of them. Patrick also did not get to New Zealand as by this time his health was starting to cause concern. During the following year he was diagnosed with a serious blood disorder and received treatment here in Australia. By mid 1987 Patrick decided to return to England for further treatment.

Our last social event together was, I recall, at the Mosman Sailing Club annual dinner held at the conclusion of the 1986/87 sailing season. Late into the evening Patrick and I were engaged in deep and meaningful conversation after the usual few hours of pleasant indulgence. I went home that night convinced that Patrick knew that he would not be returning to Australia again.

The last letter I received from Patrick was written on 28 July 1987. He indicated that his doctors were proposing a bone marrow transplant from his younger brother as a possible cure for his condition. Even at this time he was still thinking of his Australian OK Dinghy friends as he enquired about the planning for the forthcoming 25th Anniversary Dinner of the NSW OK Association and said he was sorry that he was not there with us to help.

Patrick died less than one month later on 22 August 1987.

His family in England appreciated how much Patrick loved Australia and the many friendships he had developed here. They also knew of the special relationships he had developed with the OK Dinghy people that he had met throughout the world. Patrick's elder brother, Christopher, requested that we arrange the purchase of a trophy to be donated to the Australian OK Association as a lasting memorial to Patrick and the many years of enjoyment that he had shared with us. We could think of no greater tribute than to introduce the Patrick Whittington Memorial Trophy for annual competition for first place on handicap at our National Championships and for it to be awarded to the competitor considered to be the most worthy recipient for consistent performances produced at each year's event.

In accordance with Patrick's wishes, arrangements were later made for his ashes to be returned to Australia. Years before when touring the south coast of New South Wales with Geoff Comfort, some time was spent at the beautiful town of Moruya where they visited a small cemetery situated on top of the hill overlooking the ocean at Moruya Heads. Patrick mentioned then that this was where he would like to end his days on earth when his time came. One Sunday morning in March 1988, many of Patrick's closest friends gathered at Moruya Heads and shared the moment as we scattered his ashes into the sea.

Those of us who knew Patrick well over all the years will never forget his contributions to our joy in sailing OK Dinghies. The members of the International OK Association of Australia will continue to compete for his memorial trophy at our National Championship events each year, whilst at the Mosman Amateur Sailing Club our starters' boat was simply named 'Patrick Whittington' as an ongoing tribute to a much loved OK Dinghy friend.

Olympic Champion

THERE WAS MUCH CELEBRATION IN the class when the 1994 European Champion, Mateusz Kusznierewicz, qualified to represent Poland at the 1996 Olympic Games in the Finn Class. Not only did he go on to win the gold medal in Savannah, but he shocked the sailing world by flying out the very next day to take part in the OK Dinghy World Championships in Varberg, Sweden. Perhaps the celebrations in Savannah had got to him, but after picking up two yellow flags in Race 3 for Finn pumping he decided to relax and have a social week with the OK sailors.

Cooling Beers – Peter Scheuerl

IN THE LATE 1980S AND early 1990s Agi Witt from Hamburg used to have a 1967 Mercedes Diesel, named 'Rudi'. It's debatable if the car was named after Rudolf Diesel or Rudolf Hitz, father of Karsten Hitz. On one trip the car was forced over some Alpine passes to get to some Swiss/Italian lakes for some racing, and there was some serious cooling issue, leading to total loss of cooling fluid for the motor. The owner, being a gifted mechanic, was quick to fix the issue, but a lengthy discussion started between the two sailors travelling, how much effort should be done to find water for the cooler. Eventually the beer for the weekend was used as cooling fluid, which had an added advantage. Because it was early in the year and the alcohol in the beer would also work as an anti-freezing agent.

OK Runaway – Bob Ross

Reproduced from Australian Sailing 1982.

THE COOL AND COMPETENT 23-YEAR-OLD New Zealander Richard Dodson, by far the most consistent in the fleet of 79, comfortably won the world OK Dinghy championship sailed from Black Rock YC on Port Phillip Bay.

Port Phillip was in a contrary mood. After a three-day spell of light and unreliable winds used up the layday and still left two heats to sail, the final day of racing was blown out by a 40-50 knot southwester.

So the series was decided on five heats.

Dodson's placing score, 1-1-2-8-1, for a loss of three points was far too good. Runner-up Stefan Järudd amassed 37.4 points and the Australian champion Peter Takle, 41.

Dodson indicated that his world championship campaign was hastily prepared. He had not planned on sailing at Black Rock at all until he received sponsorship help from a New Zealand company.

In winning the worlds, he fulfilled a bond to the New Zealand OK association, which he undertook when it sponsored him to attend the OK worlds in Norway in 1979. He delayed re-sailing the worlds for two seasons while he campaigned a Finn for the 1980 Olympics (he was runner up in the trials to his brother Tom).

He won the New Zealand OK championship earlier in this season.

His only other major practice this season was the Australian championship, held just before the worlds from Black Rock.

Dodson began sailing in that fertile breeding ground for singlehanded sailing, the New Zealand P-class, when he was 10. He went into Lasers and then OKs in 1977. He sailed in his first OK world championship, in Auckland that year, finishing 19th. The following year, he contested the world OK championship in Holland, finishing seventh.

1979 was his big year in OK sailing. He won the New Zealand nationals, went to Europe, won Kiel Week, then the German championship, the Danish championship and finally the world championship in Norway.

For the latest world championship he sailed a Klegecell foam/fibreglass boat, built by Gary Lock that belongs to his brother. It was on minimum weight.

Dodson said he didn't set his boat up in any special way for this series and he largely relied on his experience from previous OK sailing. "I was a bit worried I might be a bit big for the OK. I'm 13 stone, and I think the ideal weight is about 12 1/2 stone."

Dodson used a 3M Needlespar mast, and a main from Lidgard-Rudling. He felt the sail was very powerful and gave him a definite edge in the choppy conditions off Black Rock.

Before leaving New Zealand, Dodson had quite a bit of heavy-weather practice. He had done a lot of working up against his brother and cousin. "We've been competing against each other for a long time. I come from a big sailing family."

He said psychology played a big part in series racing. "When I won the first two races, Takle (third overall in the worlds) got two seconds. I was a bit worried then about what would happen if the series stayed light."

He said he always tried to go into a series with a very positive attitude. "I always try and beat my main opponents in any racing before the series. Then it's in their mind that I have beaten them."

Rick Dodson in 1982 at Black Rock.

He said the entire New Zealand team of 22 sailors was right behind him in his bid to win. "The 22 New Zealand boats were always working together. But that didn't happen with the Australians. I got the feeling they hated each other."

The defending champion, Peter Gale of Melbourne, who automatically qualified, dropped out of the world championship after very lowly placings in the first two heats. Gale had just won the world Flying 15 championship in New Zealand and had not been sailing OKs.

He had sold his boat to Melbourne 16-year-old Tony Reynolds, with the proviso that he could sail it in the world championship. Reynolds, who sailed an older boat in the first two heats, climbed into the ex-Gale boat for heat three and won it, with a brilliant last leg. Reynolds, however, had not received the necessary permission from the race committee to change boats and was subsequently disqualified.

The OK Rig: the Early Days – Jonty Sherwill

THE ORIGINAL ALL-WOOD CONCEPT OF the OK Dinghy has continued to allow anyone with basic woodworking skills to get sailing, and while advancing composite technology has allowed the class to stay fully up to date the trickiest part to get right has always been the mast and sail.

Early photos of class racing show upright stiff masts, high booms and flat sails, and with no specified mast position in the rules it seems that in 1957 our designer Knud Olsen thought it better to allow the rig to evolve. Even the 1965 edition of the OK building plans shows 'Approx 800 mm' from the bow to the front of the upper mast bearing, This is 100 mm more than a modern boat, and considering that these plans remained 'current' until 1986, first time amateur builders would have been working with less then perfect information.

The task of building your own wooden mast required greater skill than building the boat. Sourcing suitable timber, routing out the mast track and gluing up took time and patience, while planing and shaping the mast to obtain the correct bend and stiffness needed a confident eye and a steady hand. It's no wonder that masts were often far too stiff.

Knud Olsen's decision to use the Pirat class mainsail was a sensible choice. The alternative design proposed by Paul Elvstrøm would have been based on his excellent Finn sails, but by opting for the Pirat sail it allowed the use of old, low cost sails to help the class get going in Denmark. Another plus point was the emergence of the unmistakable top batten 'roach', now such a common feature of modern racing boats and dinghies. The recognised speed benefits of a 'big head' mainsail and hull chines has helped reinforce the OK's cool image.

While a good sail is essential for performance, equally crucial is the mast, and the complete freedom to experiment with stiffness, bend characteristics and position made the OK unique and appealing, allowing sailors to get a mast and sail to suit their weight. At least one UK sailmaker built this into their marketing, Seahorse Sails offering a 'Tuned Unit' with mast from Dick Larkman or Harry Millican.

To achieve better upwind speed masts became very flexible and by the late 1960s the 'hockey stick' rig was the norm at least in the UK, but change arrived with stiffer masts by Kjølhede and sails by Hamlet and Raudaschl. These were designed with less luff round to provide a boost to downwind power. Some of the new-style masts though stiff above deck were shaped to increase low down fore and aft bend and at the top shaved flat on the sides to induce sideways tip bend but still retaining leech tension.

This drive for stiffness led mast makers to look to timbers other than the more usual Sitka spruce. This included Douglas Fir (aka Oregon Pine) and even Ramin, the white close-grained hardwood more associated with modern furniture production. The one I received was splitting down the grain before I even put the fittings on so it was returned to the supplier.

My K709 at Harwich Town SC Open Meeting in 1971: In the UK Ratsey & Lapthorn in Cowes were known for their fast Finn sails, and by chance my first OK had a sail made by Ratsey, made in 1965. It had a simple curved leech and no roach at the top batten, much like a Finn sail, so it's conceivable that this is how the OK sail might have remained had Paul Elvstrøm prevailed. The photo of K709, a home built boat, suggests that the mast was 800 mm from the bow as per the building plan, but despite this and the unusual old sail the boat was remarkably quick.

By 1973 the early alloy masts had arrived, firstly borrowing technology from the Finn Class but soon other makers such as John Boyce, Proctor and LJ in Sweden joined Needlespar in the battle to produce the ultimate OK mast. The next revolution, carbon fibre masts, was still decades away and the story of that development deserves a separate article.

Once is Coincidence – Peter Scheuerl

ON THE WAY TO THE Worlds in Adelaide, Australia, in 1998, Christian Hartmann and I got to Sydney and checked into a B&B in the suburb of Ultimo, close to the city, but not the tourist center. After sleeping off a little of the jet lag, we set off to see some Sydney things. The first thing we see leaving the room was this huge person standing in the hallway, probably even appearing taller as the sun was behind his back, so we just saw the frame of the person. Just as we were saying to each other how tall some people in Australia are, the person says hello to us in German – it was Jan-Dietmar Dellas, who by chance had booked into the same B&B (none of us had pre-booked it) on the same day (we only stayed in Sydney on the way to Adelaide) – what are the chances – small world...

Two Nuts and a Trailer

NICK CRAIG HAD ALMOST RECOVERED from his colossal hangover from the celebrations the night before – which has encroached into the morning just gone – and had finally taken the wheel of his car as we reached The Netherlands, on the long drive from Skælskør in Denmark to Dunkirk in France for the late ferry back to the UK. All through northern Germany he had slumbered away the excesses of various bars after winning the 2005 OK Dinghy World Championship, his first OK world title. He had to be shovelled into the car at crack of dawn in Denmark, so we could make the first ferry at Rødby, but he had a lot to celebrate. Somewhere past Bremen he announced "hangover gone" and proceeded to demonstrate his unique driving skills like only Nick can.

All was going well until we were just coming out of Utrecht. The slip road curved round to meet another highway before heading south. Suddenly there was a deafening noise from our back end and Nick hit the brakes as the double trailer swerved left and right and we thought it would turn over. It all happened very quickly and as we came to the final juddering stop, a wheel shot past the passenger side at about 70mph straight down the motorway. We watched speechless the wheel bounced its way down the road missing all the cars it came across. At any moment we expected a huge car pile up in front of us. It finally headed for the central reservation and we closed our eyes waiting for the inevitable as it crossed into the oncoming traffic. But nothing happened. As we opened our eyes, the scene before us was normal. No pile of wrecked cars, no fiery inferno, just normal Dutch traffic.

Nick, clearly in shock, said, "What do we do now?"

Robert, "We go and get the wheel, Nick."

Nick, "Oh. Go on then."

It was then we realised that we had traffic coming past both sides at 80 mph as we had ground to a halt in the V-shaped intersection of two meeting motorways. Cars started sounding their horns, surprised at finding a dilapidated British car with a boat on the roof and two boats on the back with a trailer whose axel had ploughed a nice trough in the pristine Dutch road. The third boat was that of Jon Fish, who luckily enough had earlier flown home to sail another regatta. I told Nick to find the wheel spanners and dig out the spare in case the errant wheel could not be found while I risked life and limb crossing a three-lane motor-way, and sprinted (those were the days) off down the grassy verge.

I got to the turn in the road where I assumed the wheel had met the central reservation and exactly where I had thought it would be, the wheel was lying in the grass, looking very innocent. It was heavier than I expected as I carried it the half mile back to the intersection where Nick was waiting, having jacked up the trailer.

Can you imagine our surprise when we presented the wheel back onto the axel to find that it didn't fit? We tried several times, before the realisation set it that I had picked up the wrong wheel. The chances of there being a second wheel lying beside the road exactly where ours had landed were slimmer than slim. But it had happened. Rather than carry the wheel back to where it was found, it was dumped in the verge and I ran back down the road, further than before, to look again, but there was nothing to be found. This was quite surprising as if it hadn't landed there it must have crossed at least four lanes of busy traffic without causing an accident. The chances of that were remote. It was a complete mystery.

Back at the trailer we fitted the spare, taking two nuts off the other side. We still had 300 km to go to Dunkirk and were now rather late for the ferry and we only had two nuts on either trailer wheel. This was no problem as Nick was driving and we made it with time to spare, nuts intact.

Once we were underway we got an SMS from Jon asking how the trip was going. The answer went back: "Wheel came off trailer in Holland. Left it there." We let him stew for several hours before putting him out of his misery by saying we had just left the wheel there and not the trailer.

PART 2
Sailors and Boats

Bill Tyler's 70th Birthday Celebrations – Jan Tyler

BILL'S 70TH BIRTHDAY HAPPENED TO coincide with the prize-giving ceremony of the 2010 OK World Championship held in Wellington, NZ. Bill thought this coincidence was amazing and was quite chuffed because the event was being held in the Icon Function Centre at Te Papa Museum in Wellington and that fact was repeated many a time – to anyone willing to listen! Bill shared his birthday and cake with our NZ friend Meg (now Matt Stechmann's wife), both of whom are delightful friends met through OK Dinghy sailing. As always, everyone enjoyed the celebrations to say the least.

A birthday gift to Bill from Team Australia was a Maori talking stick, which everyone thought very appropriate. Many people have heard Bill having his say from time to time. This is the meaning behind it: "The talking stick is regarded as a staff of office that is often used by tribal elders to confer authority and punctuate speeches. The carvings represent ancestral figures and are there to protect and guide the speaker and add authority to his speech."

Like most regattas and championships that Bill competed in, they were all good excuses for us to tack a holiday on the end of competition and glorious New Zealand was no exception with three weeks driving around both North and South Islands.

Like us, our Swedish friends Thomas Hansson-Mild and his family Annelie, Maja and Carl were also driving around New Zealand and on a

few occasions we met up during our travels and enjoyed meals together. Thomas and Annelie have been absolutely wonderful friends ever since we met, when they came to Australia from Sweden for the 1998 World Championship in Adelaide. They stayed with us in Sydney for a few days during their motoring holiday in Australia after the championship and we in turn stayed with them in Sweden after the World Championship at Båstad in 2001.

Bill and I almost felt like grandparents when Thomas and Annelie's two children were born. Such was the friendship, that Bill would not only write emails to Thomas and Annelie, but sent emails to Maja and Carl while they were learning English language at school.

A truly blessed connection with a marvellous OK family and the friendship will be treasured forever. What wonderful memories over the years.

Good News – 1965

AT THE LAST MEETING OF the SAYRA. Mr. Ernie Morrison, South Africa 's leading Finn helmsman, proposed that the OK Dinghy be accepted as a National Class. For this our association send a hearty thank you. That we have an ally as well known and respected as he is a feather in our cap. It is now up to us to justify the belief in the OKs. This means more activity from all of our members. Remember, the more you sail the more notice will be taken of us, making National status easier to come by. The decision at the time of the meeting was that the problem of Nationalisation should be dealt with by a special committee and we now await their decision.

A Clean House – Thomas Hansson-Mild

I REMEMBER ONE YEAR WHEN I sailed in Kiel back in 2004. Bart Bomans won the regatta and I came sixth I think. We had decided to do some training together near Bart's hometown Antwerp leading up to the worlds in England later that year. So Bart went home from Kiel and I stayed for another couple of days since I signed up for some judging in the Olympic classes. So when arriving in Antwerp some days later and I wasn't too sure about the address and was juggling about in the middle of the old town looking for his house, when I all of sudden saw that I must be in the place. Right on the pathway stood a pile of rubbish bags and right on top it all was the Kieler Woche buckle, all ready to be thrown away. So understandably I asked him as soon as I met up with him why the prize was ready for disposal? Well, he said, I already know that I won it so why keep it to look at. When arriving further in the house I kind of realised and kind of understood why the trophy was lying in the street. Being an architect, Bart had his house clean from everything that didn't serve a purpose and kept it very down sized. It was a good meeting with a good person and good family.

When I Began – François Podevyn

WHEN I BEGAN SAILING IN dinghies, 15 years ago, I was attracted by 'old-timer' boats from the 1960s, because they were cheap (nobody wanted them any more), and almost because they are far much elegant than their modern versions. I bought some of them: 420, 470, 490, 505… with wooden varnished boom, mast, batten, centerboard, rudder, and other stuff. I also bought some full-wood dinghies: Optimist, Fireball, Merlin Rocket... (A lot of annual work.)

Eventually, I bought my first (full wood) OK Dinghy: BEL 44. At this time, I had no more space to park or store her, and I immediately re-sold to a friend, even without having sailed with her.

Less than one month later, in 2014, I met Jo and Rod Andrew-Becker

Photos: François sailed one of his OK Dinghies on an ornamental pond in the middle of Brussels, the main problem being it was only paddling depth. Photos: Christophe Gaugier

during a competition of five different English dinghies in Carnac. Since I was sailing-running-driving alone my Merlin Rocket (as well as all my other boats), they suggested me to choose the OK Dinghy, as they had. The next regatta was the European Championship in Steinhude, two months later. I bet I would be there with a new (for me) boat.

Of course, she had to be a full wooden one. I found her in France (Nancy). I felt in love. The hull and the deck were varnished. F 1053 was built in 1972 by a local champion. After he died, she slept in a hangar for 30 years, but she was still ready to compete. After a deep refresh, I met Jo and Rod again in Steinhude. During the measurement, F 1053 weighed in at 72 kg. In the strong wind, I broke both of my wooden masts. A German competitor fixed one of them with a magic glue, and I was able to finish all the races, just before those who did not finish.

Since that time, I follow Jo and Rod to many OK Dinghy events. I met a lot of pretty girls and (mainly) guys. I realised that OK Dinghy is a real family, whatever the nationality, or the native language. I'm now selling all my other dinghies, except the Merlin Rocket – but that's another story.

One of those family members gave me a bargain wooden OK Dinghy: BEL 12. I gave her to another friend, who is now restoring her in his guest room. An unknown person gave me his old OK Dinghy, BEL 131 (wooden deck and mast, plastic hull). My son (15 years old) is now competing with her. Unfortunately, a huge tree branch felt on it during a winter storm, and I have to re-deck her. A friend from Luxembourg gave me another one. I gave her to another friend. Unfortunately, she died on the highway: she took off from my car roof when driving at 100mph… Recently, a friend gave me his former wooden OK Dinghy, BEL 23. After some structural refit, she will be available to any interested person.

To be complete, and honest, since it is impossible to achieve/seek good results with an old fashioned wooden dinghy, I bought last year BEL 207 (plastic hull, carbon mast, good racing sails, and many fine tuning strings everywhere…). But, for now, I still have the same ranking.

Head Wind – Peter Scheuerl

ON THE WAY TO ONE of the first Spring Cups in Medemblik, my Peugeot 205 was fairly new and I had Agi Witt with me. Close to the Dutch border in the dark, the car was getting slower and slower, while I was nearly on full throttle, hardly making 80 kph when we should have being doing 110. As Agi is a gifted mechanic, he immediately says, just stop and I'll have a look. So I stop, and as we try to open the doors, we realise that it must be blowing something like 40 knots straight from ahead, so we let the wind bang the doors shut again without getting out, and soldier on into the breeze…

Through the Eyes of an OK Kid – Leanne Tyler

AS THE DAUGHTER OF ONE of the most passionate and dedicated Australian OK sailors, Bill Tyler, I have been part of the OK family since I was born in 1972. All the children born into the OK community have been lucky to experience a fantastic family-friendly culture. Wherever we were in the world, the children were always looked after by the extended OK family. It is a tradition I hope lives on forever.

Growing up during the 70s, sailing gave the OK kids the opportunity to make friends with children from all over Australia and the world that otherwise we would never have met. My whole life was dictated by the OK Dinghy sailing schedule determining where we spent our weekends and school holidays.

During the weekend sailing, the kids usually entertained themselves whilst the ladies prepared lunches or BBQs for the evening. The older children or one or two adults were put in charge and we were allowed to

Clockwise from top left: Bill's beloved OK AUS692 Dining with the Devil before it went to its new home with Bob Buchanan in January 2017; Breakfast time in the caravan park - Dad and Patrick Whittington, Toronto 1986; Sad end to Bill's boat - Bateman's Bay, 1981; Breakfast time in the caravan park with Patrick Whittington, Patrick Coleman and Bill, in Toronto 1986.

explore our environment. I was one of the younger kids and always gave the older kids a run for their money trying to keep track of me. Because of the OK protective atmosphere, I was given opportunities to experience life, knowing someone was always looking out for me.

In Sydney, some of my fondest memories at Vaucluse were climbing the trees, hiding in the boat shed and jumping off the boat ramp. At Mosman we climbed onto the roof of the boat shed and explored the walkway up the hill. There was a fantastic kids' playground and at night we used the delivery slide outside the exclusive Mosman Rowers' Club as our own personal slippery dip.

During school holidays I remember waking up in the dark to start the drive to a state or national championship with the boat and trailer. Great care was always taken by Dad and I to check, double check, triple check all the knots tying the boat to the trailer. Sometimes we even had 2 boats.

Regattas at Jervis Bay, NSW, were always a highlight. The Husky Pub was not only favoured by the sailors but also the kids because we could run around safely at night as the parents watched on from the balcony.

Glenelg in Adelaide, SA, was one of the best sailing clubs for kids because of the fantastic kids playroom within the club, equipped with billiard table and pin ball machines, and the fun fair along the esplanade kept everyone entertained.

During the Nationals in 1981, the kids' tent at Batemans Bay, NSW, was a hit for parents and kids alike. It just happened to be set up in the park next to the caravan park where most people were staying. Someone from the tent would walk around the caravan park collecting all the kids in the morning and the parents wouldn't see us till the end of the day. This trip was a sad ending to one of Dad's beloved OK Dinghies (see photo).

Often after races, the kids would surround the sailors and their OKs wanting to clamber aboard for a tandem sail. It was always the least exhausted sailor that would succumb to the challenge.

Once into my early teens the experiences became even more fun. The 1984 nationals in Toronto, NSW, comes to mind. There were heaps of daily activities organised by the sailing club. There was a pole climbing competition with money attached to the top of the pole. I was one of the only kids to make it to the top, so I cleaned up that day.

That evening Dad introduced me to the concept of 'Drinks on Me'. Toronto was also when I was introduced to the world of the National Competition of Indoor Games. Most of the sailors attending that evening will remember it as an extremely hilarious night. Dad and I stayed in a mobile home in the caravan park with two other sailors. That night I learnt one more huge life lesson that men snore extremely loudly after a few or more beers. Not much sleep was had that night. (This event was also highlighted in Bill Tyler's 'Memories of an OK Friend – Patrick Whittington'.)

At 14 years of age during the Nationals at Maroochydore, Queensland, Dad encouraged me to go to the movies with a junior sailor from Victoria. He was being chaperoned by his fellow older Victorian sailors (who I believed also encouraged this outing as they wanted a night off from their chaperoning duties). Upon returning to the caravan park, the Victorians, after a few drinks under their belt, decided to call our outing a date and the teasing began. The teasing continued for a couple of years whilst we were very good friends.

These are only some of my memories, but every regatta brings back memories of fun and friendships gained. All the sailors became great role models while I was growing up. They became like second fathers to me, in particular Patrick Whittington who was always willing to keep an eye on me. To see people from all walks of life coming together to share their passion and exhilaration of sailing, to see the camaraderie and sportsmanship was a huge privilege. I know that anywhere in the world I could call on an OK sailor and be welcomed with open arms.

Seeing is Believing – Peter Scheuerl

SOMEWHERE IN PEIT'S ARCHIVE THERE is video proof that Jörn Richter walks on water. It was late 1980s in Kiel Week. There was not much wind, but enough to capsize as it was gusty. Jörn Richter capsized after the gybe, his sail flat on the water. Peit gybes into the sail, so his boat sits against the mast roughly where the sail numbers are. As he's not getting off by himself, Jörn Richer climbs from the centreboard over the hull, walked along the mast on the sail (both not visible in the video, just under water) and pushed Peit and his boat towards the mast top, and off his sail. He then turns around and runs back to the hull, climbs over it onto the centreboard and rights the boat to continue racing.

1967 World Championship – Mark Gardner, US 144

I WAS ALL OF 16 YEARS old. The hull was a new balsa core version with a 6-ply 6mm deck, a sitka spruce mast and a maximum width laminated boom – state of the art for North America in 1967. At the 1967 World Championship at the Royal St-Lawrence Yacht Club, Montreal, Canada, some 70 boats attended from Canada, US, Europe and New Zealand.

In the practice race, just before the gybe mark a strong thunderstorm blew through (90mph+). The fun lasted for about three minutes, after which I managed to drop the sail and get it furled around the boom. While planning downwind under a bare stick out of the dark three boats from Sweden, sailing upwind, asked me if I had seen the windward mark? Huh? I managed to limp back to the club and inquire how they were able to sail upwind in that much breeze. Seems they raised the board and sailed on the chine. (Try to do that in a Laser.) A great lesson... in humility.

The OK is still in my backyard, unfortunately it has succumbed to a falling tree. May she rest in peace.

World's Oldest Active OK Dinghy Sailor?

MERV WAS BORN ON THE March 2, 1926 and started sailing the OK Dinghy in 1980. His first OK Dinghy had a wooden mast and boom with a Paul Elvstrøm sail. He has owned four OK Dinghies during his 37 years in the class. The latest is a Rushworth, once owned by Jim Hunt when he won the 2004 Worlds. The boat now has a Ceilidh Mast with an M18 UK North Sail.

Merv Cain at the Yarrawonga Yacht Club Anzac Day Regatta in April 2017

Merv travels each year to at least four Victorian Country Regattas where the winds are generally more to his liking and he also visits various clubs during the sailing season. He has had his share of victories on his club and regatta circuit over the years and he has a simple philosophy:

'If the wind, water and boat come together then that's OK'

Once Upon a Time in Getskär – Claes Ahlström

ONCE UPON A TIME ... there was a bunch of happy amateurs from Getskär. They had mixed successes on the race course. Or maybe not really at all ... Just because the boat was old ... or too heavy ... or too bad. Then we realised that maybe you could build a new boat yourself. Cheaply. Inspired by Max, who, with the help of his legendary boat builder father, Janne Nystedt, built himself an OK Dinghy a few years ago.

Said and done! In any case, said! Where is the mould? It turned out that the Danes borrowed it the previous winter and now it was in Copenhagen. Eventually we got it, but it looked in disgusting condition. Not only was it dissolving and returning to the motherland, the Danes had bonded wood laths on the inside railing – and failed to remove them afterwards. They were rock hard and we spent a week trying to get rid of them. By that time the Danes were not very popular.

L: Besides sailing, water sanding is our favourite thing to do. Dennis, Lennart and Max having fun. R: We made cradles to put the new and still soft hulls in. We used Peter's old boat - this night he was not here, luckily. Polyester-Lennart and Styrene-Claes.

After a few more weeks of scraping, water sanding and polishing away the worst scratches we were ready to get started. But first, accurate estimates of how much material should be used. The extremely accurate calculations led to us ordering twice as much as we needed. We started building cradles to put the still soft hulls in after the moulding.

This happened in 2005/2006 in Getskär, Sweden. We built six hulls over that winter and finished them in our respective homes. Several of these boats have been in one or more world championships. I have built three more boats after this, so I have the series: SWE 2770, 2780, 2790, 2800. I am still racing the 2800. The mould used was the original Delfs mould, the Mother of all OKs.

The Lindhardtsen Classic – Hellerup 2015

IF A MAN IS JUDGED by what his friends would say about him, then there can be no greater man – or OK Dinghy sailor – than Jørgen Lindhardtsen. The esteem and respect that his fellow sailors hold for him was openly apparent when more than 150 of them came together for the Lindhardtsen Classic in Hellerup, a celebration of his 70th birthday, which fell on Saturday, 25 April, 2015.

The idea was simple. Hold a few races and a party to celebrate the 70th birthday of a legend in the OK Dinghy class, even a legend in sailing. But it turned into far more than that. The regatta attracted 63 entries from five countries, with many more sailors flying in to just be there, and still more sending messages or calling during the evening.

The fact that the Danish fleet can muster 63 boats for a one-day regatta says volumes about the current state of the class in Denmark, but it was about so much more than that. The Lindhardtsen Clas-

L: Centreboard case in place. Carefully aligned. Boat is almost ready - we thought by that time. Next step was to cut clean the edges of fibreglass. R: Vacuum bagging. Peter's comprehensive mask misted after a while. Then he was totally wild with the roller.

L: Mat is applied on the divinycell. Suddenly it has become 'sandwich'. Rock hard bottom. Light. Fast. R: Cheers for the first hull out of the mould. Sooo nice!

L: On the third boat, Lennart realised that he forgot to put in the filter. Dennis had no mask but it went as well with the hat? R: The legendary team. From left: Lennart Hansson SWE 2768, Dennis Olsson SWE 2776, Max Nystedt SWE 2773, Peter Berg SWE 2777 and Claes Ahlström SWE 2770. Lars Hansson SWE 2775 is missing in photo.

L: Is 22 kg light enough? R: Just an ordinary day in Getskär. Lennart in his old boat.

sic drew the largest one-day fleet the class has ever seen for a long time – and it was full of current and past champions, including Lindhardtsen himself.

Jørgen Lindhardtsen was sailing OK Dinghies before most of the current fleet were even born, and at 70 years old, is still beating many of them. Jørgen is affectionately known within the fleet as the 'old man'. In fact he has had that moniker since before he was the age that most of the current fleet have now become. His longevity in the class has lengthened the sailing life of countless sailors, none of who can face giving up while the 'old man' is still sailing.

He started sailing the OK Dinghy in 1964 and won the 1978 World Championship at the age of 33. Around that time he also moved into the Finn class where he represented Denmark at the 1976 Kingston Olympics. In 1993 he returned to his first love, the OK Dinghy and won the very windy 1998 European Championship at the age of 53.

In a 2007 summary of 50 years of the best OK Dinghy sailors of all time he ranked number one in the world, the most successful OK Dinghy sailor up to that point. And he just won't stop. He has inspired more than one generation that age can never be an excuse. Even at 70 he shows no sign of slowing down, still trying to develop his rig and become better. He is a role model, an inspiration and a legend for all those who sail an OK Dinghy.

Jørgen Lindhardtsen is a classic OK Dinghy sailor. He is held in very high esteem by the whole OK Dinghy community, not just for his longevity within the class and his innate ability to sniff out every last shift and never to give up, but also for integrity on the water, which is valued by many as a guiding moral compass. His viewpoint is respected by the generations of sailors that often have to sail in his wake.

All in all the Lindhardtsen Classic was a fitting tribute to a classic OK Dinghy sailor – tenacious, resilient and modestly unassuming. Even at 70 Jørgen Lindhardtsen shows no desire no give it up. To give it up would be like giving up. He has spent almost his entire life sailing dinghies in pursuit of perfect speed. The winter seasons are now his enemy having suffered from back pain for the last few years yet remarkably it doesn't seem to affect his sailing. The pain is worse in the winter when he cannot sail. But his friends help to lift him into his OK Dinghy and when he comes ashore his back is better, even after having beaten people half his age in 30 knots.

Eight years ago he was the first inductee into the OK Dinghy Hall of Fame. He stands head and shoulders above every other OK Dinghy sailor in many ways. If he ever decides to hang up his wetsuit for the final time it will be end of an era for the class, one that began in 1964. We all hope that time will not come anytime soon.

Oldies & Wood Rule, OK? – Rod & Johanna Andrew-Becker

WE MUST LIKE BOTH SAILING and restoring old wooden dinghies, since we now have six of them. The first of this fleet was my 1964 Merlin, but keeping a crew became problematic, so when in 1991 I found the original 1962 built OK BEL 1, rotting in a dinghy park and with a 'For Sale' notice, I knew I had found MY boat.

In today's money I paid EUR 100, including a very minimal trailer, which I restored and sold for more, whilst later having a really roadworthy and perfectly balanced one built to my design. Initially, BEL 1 leaked like a sieve, so much so that I could only sail at all if there was enough speed for the self-bailers to work. So I renewed the centreboard case, transom, a large section of rear floor, plus of course all decks. I then went looking for OK Dinghy events – the very first was in June 1992 at Temse, on the Schelde near Antwerp. I was inexperienced and it was

Photos from Belgian Champs 2016, by coincidence Rod's 70th birthday

rather gusty, so I attempted no gybe but, to my surprise, I ended up winning the event when the leader, one Franz Hawer, had his rudder blade revert to kit form 50 metres from the finish line. Wow, a cup on my first event – I was hooked.

By 1993 I'd met Jo, who I persuaded to buy BEL 29, naked and sitting in a field (BEL 29, not Jo, you understand), at a pricey EUR 40, and which got pretty much the same treatment but including replacing the hog as well. At the 1995 Flensburg German champs, when the class still had the old measurement jig, we found that BEL 1 measures fine....on one side. (I can no longer remember which.) So BEL 1 is not officially a real OK Dinghy, but I have always promised not to win, and until now kept my word.

We remain stubbornly full-wood, all original fittings, old ropes etc. and for us maintaining and sailing these boats in their original condition after half a century, but still competing, is a large part of the fun. After spending hours shaving off parts of internal fillets, BEL 1 is pretty much down to weight; last time we measured (15 years ago), BEL 29 came in at a solid 83 kg, but Jo figures once she's moving, the inertia will keep her going. Paintwork has always been the handyman stores' cheapest; at the moment Jo has an acrylic finish where you clean the brushes in water – but seems to work once dry; anyway she runs into things often enough that we can't justify spending much more.

For almost 25 years we have followed a regular circuit of international OK Dinghy events in a radius of 400 km or so from 'chez nous' on the Franco-Belgian border. In 2017 the combined age of our boats and crew exceeded 240. We've seen OK Dinghy sailors come and go....but a great class.

I guess if we were interested in winning we would have got the message and given up years (possibly decades) ago, but we just like being there. My ambition used to be to get into the top half in events like Haltern, but this has become pretty much impossible as the new has replaced the old, people as well as boats, whilst I get older and stupider. We don't mind; I always claimed, very ungallantly, that I brought Jo along so as to be sure not to be last – but in the final event last year and for the first time she beat me.

This is excellent news – the class is not exactly saturated with 66-year-old women still sailing this wonderful and challenging dinghy, but we intend to be here for a while, so stick around and maybe she'll do it to you in time.

Ditch the Trailer – Peter Scheuerl

WE WERE ON THE WAY to Aarhus, in Denmark, sometime in the late 1990s, to test sails with Jørgen Holm, My boat was on the bottom of the trailer and Martin von Zimmermann's was on top.

It was pretty windy, and when we drove out of a small forest we caught a gust of wind from the side. I caught a glimpse in the rear mirror of the trailer moving strangely, and then I heard a bang on the leeward side window – it was the masts hitting the glass. Seconds later the trailer was off the car and rolled several times down a bank.

Luckily, a while later a tow truck passed by and pulled the trailer out of the ditch some 15 metres up to the motorway again. Funnily enough, the damage was pretty minor, mainly to Martin's side decks, even the masts – still alloy – survived the accident.

With some brute force the completely bend towing bracket on the trailer was bent back to something sort-of-usable and we cancelled the sail testing and headed back to Hamburg.

Luckily a chain to connect the trailer with the car is not allowed in Europe, as the damage would have been much worse if the tipped over trailer had still been connected to the car…

Re-energising a Classic OK – Jonty Sherwill

THE BACKGROUND STORY: THE BUILDERS of plywood OK dinghies are unlikely to expect their boats to last 40 years or more, but a few lucky ones do, and K 1353 'Fury' is one such boat. Launched in 1970 and built by the partnership of Harry Millican and Bill Shipsides in Barnoldswick, Lancashire, the customer was James Bridge-Butler, a London patent agent and former Isle of Man TT motorcycle racer. By this time he was an uber-keen dinghy sailor with experience in the 505 and Finn classes.

Weighing in at around 70 kg (less than the boat) James may have been more suited to light or moderate conditions but his irrepressible energy compensated and he also went to great lengths to experiment with depowering his rigs for heavy weather. This tenacious streak and technical knowledge plus a remarkable capacity to drink beer made

Old and New!

him the perfect choice when elected as OK Dinghy British Class Chairman in 1974.

Having been a flier with the RAF, James' new boat was named 'Fury' because the sail number matched the number on a 1930s Hawker Fury fighter aircraft. The boat was built to special order without sheerguards fore and aft of the cockpit as allowed by the class rules and as already tried on Herb Sweetman's 'Poison Dwarf', K 1289.

Fury was to be all varnished and by happy coincidence the builders had stock of some beautiful 5 mm marine plywood with a mahogany type veneer that has never been truly identified. This was used for the deck and topsides and the boat was finished and ready for collection early in 1970. This was just as James was planning his marriage to Charlotte and this happy distraction delayed the fitout and meant the boat's first outing was the British Open Championship at Felixstowe Ferry in early September.

It was a windy week with plenty of capsizes and in one of a rescue boats was a 16 year old, and while I never consciously spotted 'Fury' in the fleet of 100 boats I knew at once that the OK Dinghy was the boat for me. Soon after that I acquired a boat and in the following years got to know James and 'Fury', and in 2007 had the privilege of sailing the boat for the first time at the 50th anniversary event at Upper Thames Sailing Club.

Some more years past and in early 2015 I arrived with my partner Vicki at James' and Charlotte's house in Henley-on-Thames to collect 'Fury', having promised to keep her under cover, give her a coat of varnish and possibly even to sail her once a year. Having not owned an OK since 1987 the feeling was a mix of anticipation and indulgence, while Vicki was delightful despite her concern about even more clutter.

At about this time an envelope arrived in the post from my friend Tim O'Leary with a copy of the new OK Dinghy International Newsletter. This included information about the 2017 worlds in Barbados. It sounded an ideal spot for that 'once a year' sail and whether or not the idea was practical, it was at least the catalyst to get the 'Fury' refit underway.

So who were Millican and Shipsides? I knew that Harry Millican made good boats and wooden masts and that his signature piece was a lightweight laminated bow handle. Also that his untimely death by suicide in the mid 1970s was another tragic loss for the class after the death of chairman Basil Crosby in an air crash.

According to Rodney Thorne, Bill Shipsides worked at Rolls Royce in Derby, and with Colin Butler and Rodney started the OK Dinghy fleet at Burton in 1964. This fleet grew steadily to be the largest in the country with 36 boats at its peak. At what point the Millican and Shipsides partnership was formed and how many boats they built may is unclear but the legend lives on.

The refit: Renovating any wooden boat is a labour of love and one's respect for the builder grows when you see the care and attention that was put into the original construction. Keeping to a time sheet must have been tough back then and is never advisable for a refit as doing so could break your resolve to finish the job.

But when the boat in question is one of the prettiest wooden OK Dinghies built in the UK the job has to be done carefully, and where areas need to be strengthened or items replaced doing so in a sympathetic way and without adding undue weight needs careful thought.

Failure of the bottom mast step dealt a death blow to many OKs, caused either by poor engineering or more likely wet rot from leaving a boat nose down on a launching trolley. Millican and Shipsides used a neat and lightweight solution but it was clear from the amount of epoxy paste in evidence that Fury's bottom step had failed at some point.

This was confirmed by James Bridge-Butler (with Jonty, opposite) and that the repair was by the great Don O'Donnell. Don also had another hand in 'Fury' having been commissioned to fit the pretty laminated sheer guards along the cockpit sidedecks. According to Don this job was done in the middle of winter in a freezing shed.

Before starting any refit work a cradle was quickly constructed using OS2 woodchip board profiled to fit the boat either way up. 75 mm pipe insulation was fitted to the profiles to cushion the boat.

The only noticeable damage to the boat was on the port side, with a cracked sidedeck carlin and grooves on the gunwhale, probably where a port tacker had tried to muscle in at a windward mark – one can only imagine the language. The transom around the pintails had some damage plus an irregular shaped coin size hole. Apparently mice had taken up residence in the aft buoyancy chamber, confirmed by the desiccated bodies still in there.

While thinking about how to upgrade the mast step the boat was flipped over to check the 45-year-old brass rails. Complete replacement was needed but removal was not straightforward as most of No.6 x 3/4-inch brass screws had found their home and did not want to budge. After breaking the heads off two or three I tried an experiment, inserting a screwdriver in the slot of each screw and tapping repeatedly with a heavy hammer. My theory was that warming up the screws and disturbing the thread might help loosen them. Hey presto, it seemed to work.

After a day or so the boat was nearly ready for rubbing down, the other jobs being to remove the corroded Elvstrøm self bailers and Holt-Allen pintles, clearly the originals but quite badly bent and with seized bolts. A unique detail on the boat, the alloy mainsheet track that James had salvaged from an earlier OK was also removed to be cleaned up.

With varnished timber how heavily to cut back with sandpaper needs some caution. Particularly with mahogany (if that's what this is) years of sun bleaching will lighten the surface of the veneer and partial removal can look very patchy. The general condition of the wood and varnish was good except at the pin holes. First the bleached filler in each hole was cleaned out with a 2mm drill bit and refilled with specially mixed filler to match the wood colour, before rub down and varnish.

With some varnish possibly as old as the boat the decision was to 'flat back' the decks and topsides with 320 paper and retain the beautiful patina acquired over the previous 45 years. The bottom panels were taken back to bare timber where needed, and the cockpit and centreboard box needed a lot of preparation. Then using Epifanes one-pot varnish, one coat of 50/50 thinned plus two full coats were applied to all areas, allowing enough drying time so the boat could be flipped on its cradle without sticking.

If I was going sail 'Fury' I wanted to be confident that the boat would not break under the strain of my 85 kg so an all new mast step was designed and based roughly on the original concept – alloy rails bolted to one of the two original mahogany 'T' blocks but extended to a new plywood knee at the bow.

Like many if not all boats of this era the mast step was set too far aft, so this refit would allow the mast to move forward by 75 mm. Thankfully no change was needed at deck level and access to bond in the new knee and fit the new step was all done through the 270 x 110 mm mast gate hole, but my arms did take some time to recover.

The work included removing the forward T-block with chisel and hammer and cutting out the 6 mm stainless steel fixing bolt. A pattern was made of the hull shape where the new knee would sit and the area stripped back to bare timber. The new 12 mm plywood knee then glued in place with epoxy and micro-fibre fillets, then further epoxy-coating the whole area.

After a rub down two coats of white paint were applied before bolting the new stronger alloy frame in place, also screwed to the Station 3 bulkhead to share some of load. Hopefully it will be tough enough for the windiest conditions, whether that would be myself on board (highly unlikely) or someone else in the future.

OK Dinghies of this era were also notorious for getting swamped after capsizing so the other priority was to improve the buoyancy. Thankfully 'Fury' was built before through deck controls became de rigueur in the UK but the washing up bowls on elastic that passed as hatches had to go and also there was no tube between the mast compartment and the cockpit, water simply limbered through open holes to the cockpit.

After some bare wood patches had been sanded and painted in the central buoyancy chamber (using a long stick with tools taped on) a 20 mm PVC drain pipe was fitted and sealed in place. For new buoyancy covers, custom made 3 mm white PVC discs were ordered and fitted with new screw-fit hatches. With 3 x 10 mm adhesive neoprene seals around the inner edges these were fixed to the bulkheads with self-tapping panhead screws and the ubiquitous (Holt)-Allen plastic wing nuts on the inside, still unmatched for design after 50 years of production.

With this project, deciding what should remain faithful to the original and what needed to be updated was driven by practicality and admittedly some nostalgia. For example, the old bent RWO pintles were coaxed back into shape, but now fitted to a full height alloy plate covering the years of transom damage and the mouse hole.

Cleverly designed items, possibly unique to Millican and Shipsides, were cleaned up and refitted, including the brass centreboard bolt assembly that is rebated into the hull skin beneath the brass rails. Those iconic Elvstrøm bailers were de-rusted and polished up, and found to be still 100 per cent watertight when closed.

Most rewarding of all was getting to know the subtle ways these dedicated builders kept their boats light and competitive, with tapered plywood reinforcements where others might use square, and screw fastenings removed after the glue had set. Most impressive of all is that they were working without the advantages of modern epoxy adhesives, and except for the building moulds every boat would have been a new project requiring an equal amount of care and concentration.

The last jobs before fitting the centreboard (another story) and heading off to Burghfield Sailing Club for the 60th anniversary celebration was stick on the repro logos and weigh the boat. As I pulled on the tackle to lift 'Fury' off the cradle it was with some relief and a moment of pride to see the needle on the scales settle at 72 kg.

Having started my OK Dinghy sailing in 1971 with a 1965 home built boat, K 709, with the wood grain running across the deck not along to save buying more plywood, the contrast with 'Fury' is huge. The professional builders or semi-professionals, sometimes doing it in their spare time as a second job, had taken the basic class drawings and within the rules created beautiful pieces of art.

I never got to Barbados but having fulfilled my promise to 'give her a coat of varnish' it was a great thrill to sail Fury at the 60th anniversary at Burghfield. Despite the windy conditions nothing broke and to have James and Charlotte there watching was perfect.

Humbly I doff my hat to Millican and Shipsides and others like them. The legacy of their hard work is the pleasure their boats gave and the ongoing success of this superlative singlehander.

A Memorable OK Trip – Jan Tyler

IN 2010 BILL AND I drove to the Big River Sailing Club at Maclean for a regatta on the Clarence River in northern New South Wales. A beautiful out-of-the-way location to get away from the rat race of the city for a short time.

Most of the 'youngsters' set up camp by the river, but Bill and I drove a couple of kilometres through sugar cane fields to a motel for the comforts of home – our camping days well and truly behind us – I think you call that 'reaching maturity'.

A great time was had by all and thanks to the hospitality of the local sailing club ladies, no one went hungry with their fantastic food. All the children loved running around and climbing the big tree near the club house – a little bit too high on some occasions and I think there was a topple or two.

After a few glorious days away, we were about 30 km south of Grafton on our way home to Sydney when we heard a noise and the engine of the car started losing power and stopped altogether. Steam was coming out from underneath the bonnet. We discovered a split in the radiator, which of course caused further damage to everything else. Fortunately I had re-charged my mobile phone that morning so we were able to phone NRMA for roadside assistance. And another positive was that we were able to get off the single lane Pacific Highway and stop in the entrance of a property with plenty of gum trees around to give us some shade during our three-hour wait for roadside assistance – not easy when you're in the middle of nowhere.

We were towed back to Grafton but the NRMA yard was closed that Monday so no assessment could be made on the car until the next day. Fortunately over the years Bill had paid for premium NRMA membership which allowed free towing and free overnight accommodation at a motel in Grafton.

Next day the diagnosis on the car was as we thought and the motor was burnt out. So we decided to accept a tow from Grafton all the way home – us, the car, and the boat and trailer. Because the towing was free, it was the best option and how else were we going to get all our 'stuff' home?

It wasn't all that comfortable sitting in the front of a tow truck for over eight hours. With little or no shock absorbers, it bounced all the way down the Pacific Highway to our home in North Rocks, Sydney, where I arrived with a numb bum. But we arrived home safe, so that was the main thing. The tow-truck driver was a very nice fellow, so that helped with the journey and we exchanged lots of enjoyable conversation on the drive south.

Believe it or not, we went back again in 2012 for another regatta. And we stayed at the same motel again.

Age Limit in Poland –1965

THE OK DINGHY BOAT WAS 'discovered' for Polish sailors for the first time during the visit of our boys participating in 'Cadet Week' in 1963 in Burnham on Crouch, England. We got the plans through the intermediary of Mrs. Duffill mother of one of Cadet sailors visiting our Championship.

Luckily at the same time we were looking in Poland for the type of boat to be used for the boys leaving Cadet class and intending in future to sail on Finn. The first OK Dinghy has been built at the Warsaw Yacht Club belonging to the school federation. The class was 'approved' by common sailors opinion and started to grow.

The first championship took place in 1964, collecting about 20 boats. The races took place on Niegocin Lake in northern Poland. From this date we have had regular championships every year in different parts of Poland. The number of participants was about 30 boats because only a first half of districts championship participants was allowed to take part in Polish Championship. The class is concentrated mostly in three areas: Warsaw, Poznan and district Bydgoszcz but the popularity is extending very fast and now we have about 130 boats spread over the country and many more under execution.

In Poland OK Dinghy has an age limit 20 years because now the class is considered as a mid- stop between Cadet and Finn. We are very interested to develop the class and to establish International contacts. For the first time our boys have met foreign competitors in Hayling Island, the results were comparatively not too bad and it encouraged us to the further efforts. Unluckily we were long lime unsuccessful in inviting foreign crews to our events. The first sailor from abroad was Mr. Sten Marklund from Sweden who visited our 'CUP of International Faires in Poznan in 1966' and participated in races. We hope that number of foreigners will grow and we extend our hearty invitation to attend our OK Dinghy events, there is no age limit for foreigners.

Now some words about organisation. Each boat after execution has to be measured and registered because without registration is not possible to get permission for participating in regatta. The central registration list is kept till Warsaw. The class is under supervision of Youth committee of Polish Yachting Association.

Now we would like to refer to idea of developing the class among young sailors. We propose to establish the World Junior Championship in OK Dinghy. It will accelerate proper development of the class and will give the arguments for the future when will be discuss the type of boat to be officially approved by IYRU for juniors. Such Junior Championship will be for the first time in 'Finn' this year and other classes will probably do so shortly.

Call of Nature –1983 Ratzeburg

RATZEBURG WAS RIGHT ON THE East/West German border. Finding the need to answer the call of nature, Mark Fisher sailed into the empty reeds on the eastern side. A helicopter was quickly above him and they were yelling *Actung ist Verboten* at him. He was trying to tell them he was just doing his business but they wanted nothing of it and told him, all in German which he understood perfectly, to get back to the west and keep out of no man's land. It was very funny, but the worst bit was that he sailed back to the fleet. He called out to Joe Porebski before massively soiling the side of his boat. Joe promptly threw up and the rest of us nearly fell out laughing. Beers every night. There were a pile of us there with four Kiwis Greg Wilcox, Joe, and Mike and Paul Bamford, as well as the Aussies Peter 'Chocko' Jackson, Fisher, Glenn 'the duck ' Collings, Anthony Reynolds and Andre Blasse. Fisher spoke perfect German as he had a year there on a student exchange but no one found out until the night they thought their van was stolen. We all went to the police station and the cops were just laughing as Fisher was going "our van has been stolen" In the end he launched into fluent German and found out it had just been towed away as it was parked illegally. Luckily it was the cops who towed it and it was around the back. I don't think they even had to pay anything.

The week before we were in Berlin and went through Checkpoint Charlie into East Berlin. The only thing we could buy with the worthless money was a boule set. We used the coins afterwards as washers as they were aluminium. We tried to leave the duck there but he managed to escape and follow us out. There were nine of us in the van. We made

Paul Bamford sleep in it on the street so it wouldn't get stolen while the rest of us shared a hotel room for three.

We all drank beer on the way back and you were not allowed to stop so we had to slow down and pee out of the door. We nearly got arrested at the border on the way out because we were all drunk apart from whoever was driving. The guys were taking photos of the border guards and we were all killing ourselves pretending to be one another when they asked whose passport was whose. Pretty stupid really as we had no idea how serious it could have been if they hadn't just thought we were idiots.

The whole trip was like that. When we went to Denmark we had everyone in our van and made the duck drive theirs. We had 900 odd cans of beer we bought for 25c a can and got hammered playing pontoon for whatever different currency we had. They had no value; it was just a coin. There was a glamour night in the club in Aarhus continuing the game. The beers were in a big sail bag in the water. There were five of us playing and in the morning the Danes counted over 140 empty cans in the corner. Can't remember a thing about the game.

The duck won Kiel, the Germans, the Danish and the British nationals before the worlds. We kept saying wait until Leith turns up. Armit pounded the worlds and the duck was lucky we got him hammered after the first two days and he did better after that.

We bought a van in London at the van market where all the travellers and dealers went to buy and sell. It took us around 40 minutes as we grabbed it when the guy drove in. Same guy, a dealer bought it back from us afterwards. Another 30 minutes. Paid £1200 for it and sold it for £1000, two and a half months later. Then we had to pack the boats so Joe stripped it bare of all the camping stuff. I think he still has the chairs in his garage. Really was the best trip ever

From Wagon Sides to Topsides - 1995

The shape of the hull being produced by Synergy Marine in the UK in 2017 originated from a David Rose design from the mid-1990s. Rose built a series of hulls from the late 1980s, which ended up with a design for plywood/foam core hulls, marketed under the Skipper brand. They achieved moderate success, with the highlight being Bart Bomans' win at the 2003 European Championship in Warnemünde. Synergy Marine took over that mould and modified the shape slightly to produce the plug that was used to create the mould used today. This story from 1995, explains about the build process of those early boats.

THE FIRST COMPLETE BOAT THAT David Rose built was K 2036, a conventional ply built boat. That was successful enough and got him a 12th place in the worlds at Weymouth In 1989. David decided to build another boat but felt that the structure in 2036 was over engineered; yet it was only necessary to hold the 6mm into the desired shape. David had heard that commercial vehicle bodies were made light and strong by using foam sandwich techniques, but with ply to form the skins. He spoke to SP Systems who were very helpful and suggested a supplier of an appropriate foam for the core. So, anxious to build a boat that would be a bit different, Dave started work on K 2042, which employed a foam sandwich technique and won the nationals in 1990.

The hull was made from a 2mm ply, 10mm foam, 2mm ply sandwich (5mm foam at the sides). The foam used was good quality closed cell foam that would not dent and is amazingly stiff. The hull was built in a female mould, the mould was a complete hull, but the ply used was low quality interior ply.

The first mould included a transom but subsequent moulds did not have a transom as it made getting the hull out much easier. Patterns were made to enable the ply panels to be cut accurately outside the mould; one advantage of 2mm ply is that it can be cut cleanly and accurately with a Stanley knife, all joints were butt joints with no scarf joints to make long panels. Weak spots were avoided by staggering the joints in the outer skins of the hull. Once cut, the outer skin ply panels were glued and stapled in place, the joints were then taped up, and the outer skin allowed to cure before the staples were removed.

The process was repeated with the foam core, as the foam was so stiff, where it was to be formed under the bow a hot air gun was used to soften the foam before it was coated with epoxy and glued to the outer skin. On 2042 both the foam core and the inner ply skin were held in place by bags of sand while the epoxy cured. On subsequent hulls David experimented with a vacuum system to hold the panels in place. The inside of the hull was covered with an air light plastic skin and connected to a vacuum pump, however he had problems getting an even distribution of vacuum across the hull, so in the end felt that the sand bag solution was easier and almost as effective. Bulkheads and centreboard box were made from conventional single skin ply and built into the hull whilst it was still in the mould

The most difficult part of the process was getting the hull out of the mould once finished as there is a vacuum formed between hull and mould as they are separated. This was so difficult that he thought that he had glued the hull to the mould and for a while thought he would be known as Rodney Rose; however, by hammering wedges in between hull and mould it came out. In hindsight he thought that it would be easier to remove if the bulkheads were not put in place while in the mould, therefore allowing the hull to be flexed and removed more easily.

The deck of 2042 was a conventional single ply skin, put on using traditional techniques. Subsequently David prefabricated a foam sandwich deck, bending it over the deck beams to get the right curvature while the epoxy cured before gluing on to the deck beams and cutting to size.

2042 came out dead on weight. In his opinion the boat was built far too strong. (Unbelievable that, isn't it Nick?) He just kept putting the glue on, not knowing how strong or weak it would turn out. Two other boats were built using this technique, 2059 came fifth in both Worlds and Europeans and 2084, which came 11th at the worlds, each of them similar shape, but with minor variations achieved by putting shims in the mould.

David is convinced that this method of building produces the best hulls and enabled some experiments to be made with different hull shapes. They are both very light and very stiff; in fact 2084, including bulkheads and case weighed just 50lbs when built. The disadvantage is the time required to build the boat and the material costs. So much so that he does not think that the method could be used commercially if an affordable boat was the aim.

Reborn – Jean-Pierre Gailes, F 104

TO THIS DAY AND TO my knowledge, I am the only survivor from the beautiful years of the launch of the OK Dinghy in France who still sails this boat.

Of Parisian origin but having moved to southern of France, it was quite natural that my family turned to the activities of the sea.

I sailed my first tacks in September 1953 at the Neptune Club of La Ciotat, a village near Marseille, aboard a Sharpie 9m2 where I embarked a few times as a passenger. In 1957, we got a Vaurien. For three years I participated in many regattas.

In the meantime, I switched clubs and went to the Société Nautique de La Ciotat, which, for many years, was a very popular center for singlehanded dinghies. The club was mainly led by a colorful character and strong personality, Charles Divorne.

At that time Charles' two daughters sailed Sharpies, but on a trip to

Denmark in 1957, a friend of Charles, Pierre Poullain, discovered the OK Dinghy. It was a revelation and that's how the first OK Dinghies were built in France, and arrived at La Ciotat and Bendor from 1958-59 onwards.

In 1960, I received as a gift my first OK Dinghy, numbered F 104 and built by the Didier shipyard in Bandol.

I was passionate about racing, and for four years I attended most French OK Dinghy championships; it should be mentioned that we were lucky enough live near the club of Bendor, where Bernard Ricard and his father, a great patron of the club, made a dozen OK Dinghies available to the best sailors around.

At the time, the great French names in the OK series were Jean Lanza in the first place, followed by Bernard Ricard, Stany Giraud, Edmond Fabre, Alain Legrand, Hardy, Verdier, Claude Quanquard, Robert Canolle, Pierre Moulin, and also Michel Aubert, first president of the ASPRYOK. In 1964, he was followed by Daniel Dahon who made the exceptional career that we all know.

Several times I won beautiful championships, and many times I was disappointed with my results.

In 1962, I was noticed by the National Technical Director Yves Louis Pinaud, and I participated the National training camp in a Finn and then, the year after, in trials in Bandol.

In 1963, I participated in the first OK Dinghy World Championship in Maubuisson, and in spite of two capsizes I ranked 19 out of 69 entries.

By the end of 1964, I had to completely give up racing, since after the military service I began to work, naturally in a sector of the marine industry.

It was not until 1987 that I bought my first Dragon, followed up to this day by eight other boats (Boressen, Wirz, Petticrows)

In 2010, as a result of a terrible life threatening accident in my Dragon during a regatta, I somewhat abandoned participating in major events, which I considered too dangerous. At the moment I use my Dragon mainly for outings with family and friends.

Parallel to my activity as a Dragon sailor, I have owned several Stars, with which I have participated in numerous regattas in France and internationally for nearly 10 years.

Then, one day in 2015, following an unexpected meeting with the President of the French OK Dinghy Association Frédéric Lamarque, came the crazy idea to sail again the OK Dinghy, the boat of my adolescence, the boat of my loves ....

Above: Bendor 1962
Below: Svend Jakobsen (left) with
Jean-Pierre Gailes (right)
Bottom: 1963 Worlds at Maubuisson

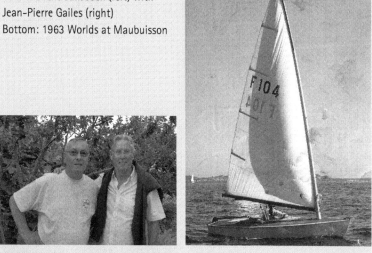

So here I am, in 2015, back in the class, at the age when most sailors have stopped for a long time.

Since then, at the helm of my OK Dinghy, I have enjoyed participating in the French events, and my performances, although average, allowed me to stand on a podium at the 2015 French Championship.

In 2016, I was physically and mentally prepared to compete in the Quiberon World Cup, which was particularly important to me, because with Svend Jakobsen, the first World Champion in the class in 1963, we were the only ones in Quiberon, to have participated in this first worlds, and the idea of being again competitor 53 years later was a symbol for me. Unfortunately, nasty sciatica prevented me from participating.

Having nevertheless made the trip, I had a great pleasure to spend several mornings with Svend Jakobsen because we were staying in the same house, and I greet very sportively the great champion that he is.

Quite naturally, I called my current OK 'Reborn', as it is unusual to get back to the OK Dinghy some 50 years later, and I kept my fetish number FRA 104 ... That is what I call a 'rebirth'.

South African Growth – 1967

THE OK DINGHY FLEET IN South Africa, now numbering nearly 60, continues to grow steadily although not at a great rate. This is not through lack of interest in the boat itself, but in the absence of a regular OK fleet at most clubs. Most sailing in the country is done on inland waters and each club caters for many different classes. OK fleets have built up mainly at Emmarentia Sailing Club, Johannesburg (where the lake is only 500 yards long), Pretoria Sailing Club, Flamingo Yacht Club, Welkom (where the lake is filled by water pumped from an Orange Free State gold mine), and inside Durban harbour. Since these centres

are separated by large distances it becomes difficult to assemble all the boats at one regatta, but we make a point of attending as many outside regattas as possible to stimulate new interest in the class.

Becoming OK – Karen Robertson

I'VE SAILED SINCE MY EARLY teens in the 1980s and it's always been a big part of my life with stints in many, many dinghy and keel-boat classes. However around 8-9 years ago I got hit by a fairly traumatic life event and I very much withdrew from sailing (and much of life) when it struck. In late 2015 I was at a friend's house and we started talking about boats and getting me sailing again. He had bought a half share in an OK (as well as him having a few other boats too) and I said something like 'Oh I've never sailed one of those before – I wouldn't mind a sail in that'.

So a few weeks later I popped down to the club where it was kept and went out for a sail in a nice onshore F3. I knew instantly I liked it and while I was only out for less than an hour, it was long enough to know that it felt really special. Unfortunately I had broken a drinks bottle holder in the cockpit and texted my friend to say thanks for the sail, and it's a lovely boat but I'd need to buy him a new bottle cage to replace the one I broke. The reply came back 'Don't worry - you can fix that when you buy the boat.' So a few weeks later I became the accidental owner of a nice OK (GBR 2122) which wasn't on any plan up until then.

During 2016 I started doing week night races at my local club in my OK but the odd thing was here was I in a boat I'd never considered before that very much spoke to me as I sailed it. Every time I sailed it was accompanied with a feeling of joy and I certainly didn't need to race to get that. Small changes brought instant feedback so even a simple hour spent sailing around on my own was as fulfilling as any race had ever been. What's more, when I did my first UK event in the autumn of 2016 I was made to feel properly welcome and part of the class from the moment I arrived at the sailing club. It must honestly be one of the most welcoming classes I've ever sailed in and I look forward to both the 2017 season and doing a mainland European event sometime soon.

Just after I bought my OK I also bought a Solo dinghy to encourage me back to do regional open meetings (there's quite a few Solos around). I only did 4-5 events but it was never a boat that touched me like the OK did and in truth I only sailed it once outside of the open events. Just

Becoming OK- Karen Robertson

after the start of 2017 I took my OK out for a short winter sail on a local Loch. Conditions weren't good, with a mixture of no-wind, cold, rain and huge swirling gusts coming off the mountains, but it was still fun, it still made me smile. When I got home I saw the Solo in the garden, looked at it and thought 'I don't want to sail you – I want to sail my OK' and so it went up for sale that night.

So what am I buying instead? Another OK of course. Not a boat to replace my current OK, but a second OK as I sail at one club mid week and another at weekends and right now I can't think of another boat I'd want to have or want to sail. It has truly stolen my heart like almost no boat ever has in my 35+ years of sailing and I can see myself sailing one until I'm too old to climb in.

So thank you OK dinghy for being one of the great hidden gems of the sailing world and thank you for getting me back into sailing when I thought I'd probably never return.

Unruly Behaviour – Perhaps the Final Food Fight

A T THE 1995 WORLD CHAMPIONSHIP 1995 at Felixstowe Ferry Sailing Club, the highlight of the week was undoubtedly the prize-giving. Felixstowe had something to match from the Europeans in Germany last year, which was an excellent evening. The formalities of the

prizegiving started the ball rolling, David Rose directing things admira-
bly again. Strangely enough, Mark Fisher (OKDIA President, Australia)
was supplied with plenty of noise and barracking when he collected his
own prize. Mark was a popular figure and he does like to make himself
heard.

The prizegiving was followed by a three course meal that ended up
being two courses with the cheese abandoned. Everyone was in such
high spirits that things got carried away a little. Ulf Brandt got a shock
when all the Brits, matched him with 'protective' clothing, for once the
Danes failed in getting the Brits wet. Björn Forslund was dispatched into
the river as profits at the bar soared to record heights. With everyone in
high spirits a live band played the night away. The party continued into
the early hours on the patio and cheese was eventually served – Martin
Jaggs turned up for the evening but fell asleep very quickly.

New supplier – 1971

A NEW SUPPLIER HAS COME ON the market in Johannesburg.
He is Tim Boorman of Qualikits. At present he is only making
complete hulls,but later hopes to be able to supply kits for do-it-your self
building. His hulls are being built of the new, to South Africa, composite construction. In this method the ply panels are held together to the
bulkheads with glass-fibre tape on the inside and outside of each seam.
This method allows boats to be built more cheaply and faster than by the
traditional framing method.

The only part fixed on conventionally is the deck as this is very
hard to tape on successfully. The method obviously produces a strong
light hull as at the last world championship in France the majority of
the wooden boats, about half the total, were of this construction. A

number of these hulls are at present being built or are contemplated. The second bit of boat-building news comes from Port Elizabeth and is strictly amateur at this stage. A mould exists for glass-fibre OKs. Tiger Tilley writes that a mould has recently been pulled from a masonite plug and is at present being finished prior to moulding a hull. We are obviously very interested in this development as, if it is successful, a fibreglass version of the OK should be a great boost to the class. We will keep you in formed of developments through this column as they come to hand. Imperial Yacht Club will have by now had their opening cruise as there is now some water in Sandvlei. Thorn de Roo tells me that he hopes to see at least three OKs sailing regularly there this season.

The Port Stephens Storm – Bob Chapman AUS 704

PORT STEPHENS IS AN IDYLLIC coastal sailing venue about two hours drive north of Sydney where for many years the annual Port Stephens Sailing and Aquatic Club Regatta, raced on Salamander Bay, was a must do for the NSW OK Dinghy Association, a great weekend away that ticked all of the boxes for OK Dinghy sailors.

The regatta held over the weekend of the 17-18 November 2001, attracted approx. 70 entries, made up of Lasers, OK Dinghies (15 entries), 505s, B14s, Hobie Cats, the odd Flying Dutchman and a couple of Lightweight Sharpies – all there for some fun racing on a great stretch of water, with family friendly facilities and close proximity to suitable post-race watering holes.

The two races on Saturday were sailed in a fresh north-easterly sea breeze, as per the brochure, fast rides and close racing throughout the OK Dinghy fleet. Sunday was a different story, two races in a warm, erratic northerly land breeze that provided some testing light air racing. Another feature on Sunday was the appearance on the western horizon of an interesting cloud formation that indicated the possibility of an afternoon thunderstorm.

This cloud formation became a serious concern during the last race as it developed rapidly into a large, menacing shape with a sinister green tinge that was heading our way. Needless to say by the end of the last race everyone was keen to get back to shore and off the water.

The storm hit, with OK Dinghy sailors fully occupied getting sails down, boats onto trolleys then up to the boat park or just hanging on

Above, taken on Saturday from the boat park prior to racing and looking east towards the course area as the sea breeze begins to build. Note the trees to the left northern side of the park.

Below, taken Sunday, post storm, to show the emerging story of retrieving Peter's OK Dinghy.

to their boats to stop them being blown away; some were caught-out on the water and rode it out on their upturned hulls. For some very tumultuous minutes the boat park was a crazy mad scene of ferocious wind, flying debris and torrential rain. Then it passed and everyone emerged from their respective retreat. It was a bewildering sight, damp, messy and somewhat surreal.

As we started to take stock of the situation Peter Horne emerged looking dazed and bewildered.

"Where's your boat Pete?"

"Over there, under that tree," indicating the pile of debris that used to be a tree.

"Where were you in the storm?"

"On the ground next to my boat. I got knocked down by the tree."

"Are you all right?"

"I think so. I was able to crawl out."

This was followed by a lot of head shaking, disbelief, and then the daunting prospect of how to retrieve the boat and what condition would it be in?

With help from a neighbour in providing some bush saws and the determined efforts of quite a few people the boat was located and eventually extracted. Absolutely no doubt the boat saved Peter from serious injury (another tick for Mr Olsen's wonderful little boat) and considering the possibilities, the damage to the boat wasn't all that bad – the mast had broken at the deck along with some serious damage under the mast step where the alloy trolley had collapsed.

The NSW State Championship was scheduled for the following weekend, prior to preparations to send boats to the OK Dinghy Worlds in Napier, New Zealand. Class stalwart Bill Tyler immediately offered the better of his two well performed boats for Peter to use as a replacement – a wonderful gesture and typical of Bill. Peter's boat was eventually repaired, with no appreciable problems and went on to perform the same as ever.

Port Stephens – perfect one day, unforgettable the next.

The Storm

A subsequent search on the internet provided the following new item. "Hunter hit by severe thunderstorms with Tornadoes. A downburst produced winds in excess of 75knots (140km/h) causing moderate damage in a path that was no wider than 5km. Salamander Bay, Corllette, Tomaree, Nelson and Shoal Bay were the worst affected areas. The most interesting phenomena that occurred when the storm passed through these areas were the tornadoes that formed across the water and then travelled over the land. It is uncertain whether the tornadoes may have been gustnadoes. Gustnadoes are classified as tornadoes as they are a rotating column of air, but technically are not tornadoes. Most of the damage that occurred was typical for wind strengths between 65-100 knots (120-180 km/h), however, the winds may have been slightly higher than this in some places. "

From Båstad to Kiel – Peter Scheuerl

VINETA WAS A 1978 ONE-TONNER, built in the US for a German owner and was used for many offshore races including the Fastnet. Over the years the boat was only very slightly made more comfortable for cruising, but was fun to sail and the owner always preferred it being sailed by someone rather than sat in the marina. So he lent it to me to use as accommodation at the 2001 World Championships in Sweden.

I picked it up in Copenhagen with Martin von Zimmermann and sailed it north to Båstad in a day. Apart from the wind picking up quite a bit for the last few miles, this was a nice trip.

Sailing it back to Germany would be a bit longer, but the opportunity to have a nice few days sailing trip through Denmark's Baltic was enticing enough for a few OK sailors to spontaneously join in and have a nice cruise.

The first problem to solve though was, that Christian Hartmann had driven three OKs up to the worlds: Martin's, his own and mine, so that Martin and I could sail the yacht up. Unfortunately Christian's insurance was bound by several conditions, one was that only he or his partner registered with the insurance company was allowed to drive the car. So a few phone calls later, Christian and Martin were listed with the insurance as partners living together in Berlin – Martin was living in Hamburg and I don't think either ever considered a same sex relationship. Christian especially was more troubled with some female partner(s) around that time and during the whole trip was more often on his mobile texting than sailing the boat.

So a team of Heather Goody, Jule Hofmann, Alistair Deaves, Greg Wilcox, Christian and Peter set off after the worlds for a nice cruise down the Baltic from Sweden to Germany.

Of course apart from the Germans on board – which was close to nothing – nobody except Peter had any foul weather gear; but it was summer and it would be fine.

Except the first day it wasn't exactly, a strong westerly front with pretty low temperatures for summer had us beating into quite some rain and waves.

So everybody got decently wet, and we discovered that the deck was slightly separating from the hull under the load of a winch – which made the bunk below it quite wet as well, and I think some people even changed colour slightly and weren't very keen on food for a while. Also some people fell on top of each other with ribs cracking and making

one crew member useless for any task which would need any strength – of course cooking and fetching beers doesn't need much strength, and someone has to do it...It was the perfect start for a nice summer cruise.

So instead of going all the way to Copenhagen, to avoid mutiny we stopped a little further north in Helsingborg...*[Helsingør in Denmark is the one with the famous Kronborg Castle – the one known from Shakespeare - Helsingborg is opposite in Sweden.]*...where you can't really see any castle (-borg) from the sea.

Luckily the Vineta had a proper heater, so after starting that, making some hot drinks and food and getting all our gear reasonably dry in the strong breeze again, the morale went up and the beer reserves went down.

We had perfect cruising conditions over the next few days, with sunny, warmer days and a nice breeze on the light side. On the second day we passed through the then relatively new bridge connecting Denmark and Sweden and down the Sund, passing Copenhagen, and eventually turning right into the small channel to the south of Denmark's main island and some smaller islands south of it.

That night in Stubbekøbing the weather was nice enough for having dinner in the cockpit and we had a long night with many tales. The next day brought flat water and light wind, and under gennaker we slowly tracked along, Christian showed his cooking skills mixed with the locally famous hot dogs (only Danish hot dogs are real hot dogs).

We had to make hard decisions which versions of the hot dogs were best; whether it was the port-dogs or the starboard-dogs escapes my memory. The mixture of British, New Zealanders and Germans on board certainly led to the creation of words, which made their way into common language.

Apart from scaring some other yachties in Svendborg – we certainly didn't bring the 'nice looking bourgeois yachtie' to the mix – we did a pretty nice docking manoeuvre into a space about 1 metre longer than the boat without destroying (or even touching) the push or pullpit of the boats ahead or astern.

The last day on the way to Kiel was spent with traditional big boat fun, like swinging on a halyard from bow to stern.

Overall it was a really nice, and for most on board spontaneous, trip and a perfect showcase for the Baltic. The first day showed that it can be rough, while the rest showed how many small fishing ports and villages there are, how lovely cruising in light wind and no waves can be, and of course how much fun you have sailing with some OK sailors on the same boat – even though the cruise turned into a race whenever there was any other boat around, and there are quite a few in summer on the Baltic.

Australian Dominance in 1998

ROGER BLASSE FIRST CAME TO prominence in OK Dinghies back in 1986 with his first National Championship as a 19 year old. Several Nationals titles, and a stint in Sharpies, a top 10 place in the 1990 worlds, culminated in his prior best being a close third in the 1994 Napier New Zealand Worlds to class guru New Zealander Leith Armit and subsequent Olympic Finn Gold Medallist Mateusz Kusznierewicz.

Being a technical pioneer in the class has always been a Blasse tradition. He was amongst the first to use the multipanelled hard cloth sails developed by Gale and Rimmington in Melbourne, built his own boat to his own design, and is now using the maximum head G&R sails recently developed and used by the top five Australians.

This technical foresight, combined with flawless boathandling skills and fitness levels combined to bring Blasse success at Glenelg.

Most other Australian competitors used very similar gear to Blasse's, with G&R hard sails and the usual Needlespar or Goldspar masts. Hulls tended to vary, with the Delfs, Botterill C&T, original Comfort & Taylors and old Botterill hulls all prominent, alongside Blasse's self built creation. The G&R sails tend to be flatter than conventional cross – cut sails, with the lightweight yarn-tempered cloth keeping them flat into the higher wind ranges, where they come into their own.

In typical OK Dinghy self-policing tradition, protests hearings were few, although 720 degree turns were plentiful. General recalls were generally limited to one per race due to the rapid use of black flags after the first recall in all starts. This resulted in a number of competitors taking early showers in a few heats, but certainly kept the racing on schedule in fairly trying conditions.

The New Zealanders, long time Southern Hemisphere dominators of the class came with 15 boats, their National Champ and big claims, but only managed to get one boat, new OKDIA Junior Champ Daniel Bush into the top 10. The New Zealanders, despite new boat development and widespread OK activity, have tended to follow Australian trends since the 1994 Napier Worlds, rather than lead development. An observation was that the NZ produced sails were too deep to perform in the heavier stuff, whilst giving no firm advantage in the light, while the ones using G&R sails were behind in fine tuning and finesse of the new style gear.

The Europeans were in Adelaide in force with one full container from Britain, and two from Germany and one from Denmark, which included boats from Belgium, Poland and Sweden. Karsten Hitz of Germany, a class veteran of many years finished a very solid third, only carrying one place outside of the top 10. Anders Andersen of Denmark, Hedley Fletcher from the UK, 1978 Champ Jørgen Lindhardtsen from Denmark and Jonas Persson from Sweden rounded out the top ten, Andersen the only other European besides Hitz to appear a threat to the Australian dominance.

Many Europeans sported British Ullman sails, a deep, tight leached monster that had awesome speed and height in the light stuff, but quickly became a handful in any sort of breeze. The ubiquitous Danish Green sails were probably better performed in Adelaide, appearing to be a better all-round proposition. The Europeans, despite being attracted to Glenelg with the promise of big seabreezes were probably glad there were not more of them. A quote from one British competitor, (after winning a rather shifty, tricky morning heat in the Australian Open Champs sailed beforehand) was, "where I come from, this is as good as it gets".

The ongoing influence of the Olympic Finn champ Kusznierewicz was seen by the continued good showing of the Polish competitors at the Worlds. Poles won races in both the Worlds and the Aussie Champs beforehand, and showed that, with a bit more consistency they can be a real force in OK Dinghy sailing.

The fledgling West Coast USA fleet was also represented at the Worlds, in a development that must bode well for the future of the class. Although there have been some boats sailing in Canada for some time, the potential of the US, regarded there as an 'old European class' will add considerably to the classes appeal. Competitors from India were also present, and whilst there presented a proposal for a future world championship to be sailed in Goa.

The ongoing success of the OK Dinghy can be attributed to number of different factors. Firstly, it is not an Olympic Class, so it avoids the expense and class jumping of the Finn, but is close enough in sailing skills and style of the Finn to offer the single handed athlete a challenge. Being smaller than the Finn, it also offers sailors closer to the population average mass a chance, although the demise of weight jackets has meant 75 kg types may find it tough. It is not an easy boat to sail, and a very difficult boat to sail well in a breeze. Once tamed, a sense of accomplishment tends to keep those in the class. The OK Dinghy is very cost effective. Many of the boats at the worlds were 10+ years old, and it made no noticeable difference to performance compared with the brand new boats. John Gibson's Botterill hull was 17 years old and finished fifth. Masts and booms can last 20 years, and the class has so far resisted moving to carbon spars on cost grounds, finding that the existing UK Needlespars and Australian Goldspar rigs more than adequate, and although expensive upfront, proving to have great longevity. Sails are relatively cheap, and can last a couple of seasons, whilst providing tuning and development challenges.

The best thing about OK Dinghies, and the most important factor in keeping competitive sailors in the class is the spirit of the class. The self-policing nature was mentioned above, and it is a real feeling of 'let's get together, race hard but fairly, and I'll see you in the bar for a beer'. A fairly simple philosophy, but obviously popular, considering that three other countries besides Australia required selection regattas to limit the numbers of those who wanted to come. Soren Krause, international judge and jury chairman summed it up when he said, to paraphrase 'the OK Dinghy class has a really good thing happening – all of you need to work hard to keep it that way.'

And the Melbourne OK sailors, long regarded as talented but flawed rebels in the Victorian sailing scene, standing at the Black Rock YC bar, would drink a toast to both their fourth World Title and the sentiments above.

Espresso Express – Peter Scheuerl

MARTIN VON ZIMMERMANN AND I travelled to many events together, and often the trips home after a full day of sailing on a Sunday night dragged on quite a bit. Once coming back from somewhere east of Hamburg in the middle of the night, with no service station or restaurant around, we decided to cook some coffee with the one-flame camping gas cooker and the stove top espresso machine of mine. But that would mean stopping for around 15-20 minutes, so we decided to make the coffee in the car while driving. I still admire Martin's skill to balance the cooker with the coffee maker on top between his feet in the foot well, while we drove at 100 kph on the motorway, and I'm sure some of the truck drivers we passed wondered what about the blue flame-glowing light in the car.

Driving in Europe – Robert Deaves

TRAVELLING WITH NICK CRAIG IS always an interesting experience. We were on our way to Warnemünde Woche in 2007 in his clapped out old car, with two boats on the back, one on the roof and Jon Fish in the back seat. I seem to remember that one side of the roofrack was secured by a rope through the inside of the car, not an ideal situation for a 700 km drive. Now, in those days, Nick never liked to drive slowly – I am sure he is more careful these days – so he was overtaking every vehicle on the road going through Holland, trying to make closing time at the bar at Warnemünde. One particular Dutch driver took affront at this and passed us, before pulling in and braking in front of us to slow us down to a sensible speed. Nick didn't like this so pulled out and passed him. The Dutch driver did the same again, slowing us down after overtaking. Then Nick did the same. This happened four or five times before the Dutch driver gave up and sped away into the distance.

About 10 km before the German border, a police car came past and signalled for us to stop. We pulled over into a service area and after a few pleasantries, the policeman asked Nick to step out of the car. He informed Nick that there had been a complaint to the police that a British car towing boats was out of control and seemed to be driven by someone under the influence of drugs. There were stifled sniggers from within the car as Nick was forced to walk a straight line and take a breathalyser test, before we were allowed on our way. Nick drove sensibly for the next 10 km, to the border, before putting his foot down and we just made the bar in time for a few beers.

Nick's propensity for speed is only matched by his dislike of lighting boards and any sort of preparation. A few years before, on the way to Kiel Week, again at breakneck speed to make last orders, we were pulled over by a policeman near Osnabrück in Germany, by helpfully flashing a 'pull over' sign on the back of his motorcycle. He informed us that not only did we not have a legible number plate on the lightboard, but also that none of the lights were working, and we had to stay there until dawn before proceeding.

We explained the urgency of our arrival in Kiel for a competition and eventually the policeman relented and told us to drive slowly to the next intersection where there was a service station, which might be able to help. So he rode behind us, while we carried on for a few km looking for the service station, all the time resisting the temptation to try and lose him in the dark. Once at the service station, Nick's technical and wiring skills came to the fore as we opened the lightboard socket only to find none of the wires attached to the terminals. Nick did manage to find a marker pen to make a number plate, but was completely stumped about the wiring.

Nick writes later in this book about being lucky, and as luck would have it, the next voice we heard was in a broad Birmingham accent asking if we had a problem and needed any help.

It turned out he was a car mechanic working in the middle of Germany and was still there late at night. We bought him a coffee and he set to work mending Nick's rather sick lighting set. About an hour later we were on our way again. We missed last orders, pitching our tents in dark in the small hours, which luckily turned out to be as close to the launch ramps as it was possible to get.

30 Years 'Aft the Mast' – Henry Metcalfe

Henry Metcalfe was President of OKDIA from 1985 to 1990.

THE FIRST TIME I SAW OKs sailing is irrevocably etched in my mind; it was 1964 at Waldringfield and I was a young schoolboy. I was immediately impressed by their lightness and speed. Four years later I had grown a bit too big to get a Cadet and to my great delight a teacher suggested an OK.

My first OK number K 72, a sturdy machine, was soon acquired from a farmer in Woodbridge and I spent the summer sailing her including Deben Week [*A week of racing on the River Deben on the east coast of the UK.*] Although I was soon competent I was only competitive with boats of a similar age and the reason was very apparent when I weighed her: she was about the same amount over the minimum weight as her number, about 70 lbs (32kg).

The next year I dipped into my savings and ordered a new boat from Seamark Nunn then one of the top UK builders. Soon K 1317 was built and I was much more competitive with a Seahorse sail and Larkman mast. This was built from a single section of Sitka Spruce which was split and re-glued in reverse so as stop twisting and warping which could be an issue with timber masts in those days. The height of tuning sophistication then was a Seahorse Tuned Unit when the mast was supposedly match to the sail. I discovered that the reality was that the first time the sail met the mast was when it was delivered to the customer so I saved myself circa £12 by not having a 'tuned unit' and my sail fitted the mast just as well as my friends who had ordered 'tuned units'.

I have many happy memories of sailing at Waldringfield with seven or eight friends in the summer holidays – we had no coaches in those days and were entirely a 'self-help' group. Our OK sailing skills improved but not as quickly as they would have done if we had had some coaching. I remember that the 'pundits' in the main were very guarded about the secrets of their speed and reluctant to tell us anything about tuning.

Deben Week became the main warm up for east coast sailors for the National Championships and the OKs regularly had a fleet of between 20 and 30 boats. In the late sixties and early seventies its winners included Jem Goddard, Mike Richardson and Peter White. From the mid-seventies onwards the 'new kids on the block' took over fight for the podium position with Robert Farthing, Jonty Sherwill, Andy Gilmour and myself each winning overall in these years. Many visitors such as John Derbyshire came from further afield as its role as a warm up regatta for the Nationals was recognised.

My first open meeting away from the River Deben was a successful foray to Leigh on Sea where I finished sixth out of 48 boats. At that time I was setting the mast up nearly vertical which was fast in light winds, especially downwind, but not so good upwind when the wind increased. I was fortunate that this was a light wind event and even more fortunate in the second race when I arrived at the first mark at the end of the windward leg in the top 10. I moved up to sixth on the first reach. The wind then backed every time I got to the new leeward mark so we had three running legs before the race was shortened and I had moved up to third behind Wendy Fitzpatrick, at that time deputy Editor of Yachts and Yachting, in first place. That evening I overheard a couple of the 'pundits' of the time grumbling to each other that 'a kid with a near vertical mast had gone much faster than them but as their rigs were set up with more rake they would have him tomorrow in the more normal races they expected with more windward legs and fewer runs.

With the lack of coaching and little sharing of tuning information, observation plus snippets of overheard information such as this were all we had. I learnt fast and the next day I put some rake in my mast and went consistently well with top six results in every race including beating the 'pundits' who I had heard in the tea queue the day before.

Felixstowe Ferry 1970

MY FIRST NATIONAL championship at Felixstowe Ferry in 1970 was a bit of an eye opener. The forecast was for windy conditions and that was enough for a number of helms in the fleet of 128 boats to get their planes out and start tuning their masts. Wood shavings swirled around the dinghy park and clearly some overdid it as there were a large number of broken masts that week. Many a helm claimed that they had gone the fastest they had ever gone just before their mast broke.

The class was about to witness one of its periodic step changes in development that marked its evolution from time to time.

The vogue at that time in the UK was for very flexible 'hockey stick' masts that hinged at the bottom, matched up with sails with loads of luff curve cut into them. Mike Richardson from Seahorse Sails had won the 1968 Nationals at Kippford with this type of rig which was very fast upwind but not so good offwind. At Felixstowe, the Danish boat builder Steen Kjølhede romped away offwind while holding the best of the UK boats upwind. His mast was stiffer and beautifully built in multiple laminates of different types of wood and it was matched with a Hamlet sail

British Nationals at Felixstowe Ferry in 1970. L-R: Richard Wilde, Jem Goddard, Daniel Dahon, Steen Kjølhede, John Dawson-Edwards

with much less luff curve but more seam shape cut into it which fitted perfectly. The result was that the mast didn't have to be bent so much to achieve the optimum set and the drive was delivered into the hull rather than into bending the mast. Another element in Steen Kjølhede speed was a super lightweight stiff hull, with all the weight concentrated in an oversized piece of timber under the traveller. Needless to say Steen won the Open British Championship from Frenchman Daniel Dahon, Richard Wilde and British champion and Jem Goddard.

Following this championship Seamark Nunn started importing Kjølhede masts with matching Hamlet sails. I ordered one and all I had to do was give my weight in kilos and a beautifully matched rig was duly delivered the following month which did what you would expect from a tuned unit.

There were 110 entries for the 1971 Nationals at Sussex Motor Yacht Club, Shoreham and there were several top Finn sailors in the fleet including Chris Law, then the best single-handed sailor in the UK. My confidence grew as I realised that I had good speed both up and down-wind and I was never out of the top 20. My own downwind speed was pretty good but Dick Batt shot past me as if I was stationary. This was the first time I had seen pumping downwind and to keep up I copied him and was soon also shooting along. There were several top overseas com-petitors in the fleet but not all did as well as expected. The French came in force but the runner up from the previous year Daniel Dahon crashed into the late twenties (perhaps the south coast beer was not as much to his liking as the east coast beer). His countryman Monsieur Leonard came seventh and Monsieur Planchot drew with me 14th=. Chris Rho-des finished first ahead of Mark Loughborough and Chris Law in what was a high scoring series with many snakes and ladders.

I took a break from OK sailing to sail 505s and returned to OKs in 1975 acquiring a very nice boat from Didge Everett of Harwich Town SC. She was one of the John Cook built hulls that were fast and cheaper than many OKs at the time. John was a house builder who just built OKs for fun at the weekend, and kept costs down by using marine ply without any 'Fancy Dan' mahogany sapele facing. He utilised a development of the 'stitch and glue' method first pioneered in the Mirror dinghy. The colour of the ply in these lightweight hulls soon weathered where it was varnished and my boat was nicknamed the 'Flying Tea Chest' in recog-nition of its colour.

By the time I returned to the class in 1975 another 'sea change' in mast development was taking place after a change in rules to permit metal masts. At first they were over specified and more like telegraph poles and wooden masts were still competitive. However the rival manufacturers of John Boyce on the east coast, and Needlespars in Warsash, steadily developed their aluminium masts, which were soon to become faster and more consistent than wooden masts. The 3M from Needlespar was my favourite mast and I sailed with them for over 15 years. Needlespar made variations with blue tops and red tops but to be honest the black tops were better and for all we knew the biggest difference between masts was the colour.

Incidentally years later at the 1980 Open at Harwich Town, Ian Godfrey quite accidentally demonstrated the robustness of the Needlespar mast. On his arrival Ian proceeded to drive under the height restriction bar at the entrance to the car park. Unfortunately, the angle at which the mast was fastened meant it went over the top of the bar while the boat and trailer went underneath. There was much shouting and gesticulating by those assembling their boats in the car park as they saw what was happening, but to no avail. Ian who was keen to show off his motor revved the engine more but barely moved forwards. He eventually turned the engine off and got out to see why he couldn't get into the car park. He turned ashen face as he realised the error of his ways and saw the new banana bend he had put in the mast.

After some time, Tim O'Leary suggested to the inconsolable Ian that he try and straighten the mast. Tim set up a couple of park benches which the local council had thoughtfully left for such a purpose and soon the combined weight of half a dozen OK sailors sitting at strategically critical places on it and carefully bouncing on the count of three soon had the mast more or less straight. The last laugh was with Ian who went on to win the open meeting.

The 1975 Nationals held at Harwich Town Sailing Club were eventful in many ways. There was a bit too much drinking on occasion which gave rise to some amusing incidents. One evening a group of about 40 discovered the Dovercourt boating lake with its fleet of paddle boats unsecured for the night. Of course some of the group had to have a go and some improvised racing started with much cheering on from the spectators. After 15 minutes the sound of a police siren was heard rapidly approaching. Those afloat speedily paddled for the pond edge and all scarpered quickly leaving one unfortunate to face the music. This was Chris C who had the misfortune to have selected the one boat with one useless paddle. When the police arrived all they found was the unfortunate Chris going around in circles at high speed. He eventually made it to the shore and was let off with a stern ticking off. This championship wasn't so good for me as I suffered from a 'sporting injury' to my knee after a collision with an anti-tank two-meter cube of concrete which finished the week for me. The week was won by Dick Batt from Chris Rhodes and Julian Kettle.

Ladbroke Grove YC

AT THIS TIME Jonty Sherwill and I commenced sharing a flat in Ladbroke Grove, London and our flat always seemed to have visiting OK sailors staying. We had been tuning partners for some time along with various others including Tim O'Leary, Andy Gilmour, Jeremy Young, Tui Scott from New Zealand and Charles Williamson. I also became Class Chairman and for several years the midwinter committee meeting, coinciding with the London Boat Show, was held at the Ladbroke Grove Yacht Club as our flat became known. These meetings were planned to end in the early evening in time to have a few beers before proceeding to a restaurant in Notting Hill. There was considerable consternation on one occasion when at the end of the meeting we couldn't open the door to go to the most important part of the proceedings. There was no other way out as the flat as it was on the third floor. When brute force failed to open the door we were becoming so concerned that consideration was given to calling the fire brigade to get us out with a turntable ladder. At that point quick thinking by yours truly came to the rescue. I got everyone to move from the centre of the room to the walls and sure enough a 2 cm gap below the door appeared and it swung open, releasing the meeting.

The 1976 National Championships were held at the very hospitable Elie & Earlsferry Sailing Club. By this time our long boat tuning sessions were paying dividends, particularly for Jonty, who took the sensible but unusual step for an OK sailor at that time of only drinking orange juice during a championship (since denied). A further development was also on the nutritional front. Races were still long then with one or two a day of an average length of at least two hours per race. The choice of snack was limited compared with now with most of us eating things like multiple Mars bars. This completely put me off Mars bars and to this day I cannot bear them. Jonty developed the 'Mars bar sandwich' spending what seemed like hours slicing up as many as six bars to go into sandwiches for the day. I and others tried eating copious amounts of dextrose tablets which caused some hilarity as we powered to windward foaming at the mouth. The overall results were Chris Rhodes, from Jonty Sherwill and Dick Batt.

FELPHAM **1977**

THE 1977 EUROPEAN Championships hosted by the UK at Felpham were eventful to say the least. The measurement saga was just the beginning of the 'fun'. The event commenced with a measuring marathon in which many boats from one overseas builder were initially quite rightly thrown out. To even the most casual observer they didn't look like OKs with so much curvature in the bottom panels and topsides that the chines were barely visible. The resultant curvature meant the panels could be built much more lightly and weight concentrated in the centre of the boat with for example an oversized beam under the traveller. Fortunately, the measurement was overseen by Elizabeth McMillan an RYA appointed measurer, who was completely independent from the class's technical committee. She was a delightful, charming and firm Scottish scientist whose interpretation of the rules was precise and accurate and she wouldn't be swayed or bullied by a bunch of pesky OK sailors. After many telephone calls to both the builder and the original measurer, the owners of these boats admitted defeat and set about cutting the panels next to the bulkheads into which a saw blade was inserted to cut out the curve from each bulkhead. The panels were then glued together again and this time passed the measurement.

In the following year the class tightened up its measurer appointment procedures and in Britain Elizabeth McMillan was invited to oversee the measurement of the next two international events held here in 1983 and 1989. From then on, the build rule observance in the class was much improved.

Other events in the week included the camp site we were staying at being completely flooded out by a flash rain cloud to the extent that everyone on it had to find alternative accommodation. The younger members of French team spent the championship getting into trouble with everyone – their coach and team leader, Daniel Dahon, and his wife, the club, the club's neighbours and the local police.

In a different vein a then young Mike McIntyre earnt everyone's respect for working through the night to repair his boat after serious structural failure and then did very well in the racing next day despite having had virtually no sleep.

The week was blighted in the main by very light winds and there was a serious risk of not getting in the minimum number of races (five) required to make it a championship. On the penultimate day we went afloat for an 8:00 am start for the first race. This race was successfully completed but then the light and fickle wind 'boxed the compass' throughout the rest of the day. One race I particularly remember turned into a run half way up the first beat. The fleet ran into the former 'wind-ward' mark in a straight line with 70 odd boats calling for water on the outside boat. Luckily the race officer abandoned this race. After many re-starts we eventually got three races in that day. The final race was the most dramatic starting at dusk and with the final beat in pitch black with the Committee Boat orientating the fleet by its profusion of floodlights. As we finished we were told to sail towards the row of car lights shining out to sea from the shore. We eventually got ashore after 11:00 pm. It was remarkable that everyone came in at the correct place as there were several different sets of headlights pointing out to sea. For the race officer the 'fun and games' were not over. He was reported by a German competitor to the police for 'endangering lives' and had to spend some time answering their questions that night.

The next day we were up for another early start and the final two races were completed on time, with Alex Hagen from Germany winning from Dick Batt and Thomas Ojelund, of Sweden, while Jonty Sherwill gave notice of what was to happen in the next year coming a very creditable seventh.

After the previous year's Europeans the 1978 National Championship hosted by South Shields in 1978 was a 'doddle'. We camped next to the club which had its plus and minus sides. In the later category was a particularly persistent penetratingly monotonous flat toned bell on the nearest channel buoy in the mouth of the Tyne. This was soon christened the 'bell of doom' and kept many a restless sailor awake for half the night. It was just the excuse others needed for a final nightcap or two before staggering uncertainly off to their tents. Among other 'delights' were the high levels of pollution that flowed out on the ebb tide. Despite this and various other pre-championship events the friendly South Shields Club ran an excellent Championship which Jonty Sherwill won from Alastair McMichael and Clive Evison.

Jonty's victory celebration was memorable, particularly the visit to

Plymouth National Championships in 1979. L-R: Henry Metcalfe, Patrick Whittington (Australia), Peter Gale, wearing Henry's glasses as he thought they would make him look more like a professor (Australia) and Geoff Woollen.

the 'chippy' where he asked in a slurred manner for "one of everything"! The next morning the 'bell' had its revenge on him.

The 1979 Nationals at Mayflower Sailing Club Plymouth were memorable for me in many ways. I had just become engaged to Maureen who was to take over from Judy Palmer as secretary to the class the following year. Judy had ably served the class for most of the previous decade.

One incident sticks in my mind from either the second or third race. The Plymouth Sound was busy with both naval and commercial shipping for which you had to keep a sharp lookout as well as your opposition in the other OKs. In this race I was running with the leading group of boats spread across the course. I was particularly concerned about John Derbyshire and Ian Godfrey in that race. We were running parallel to each other about 50 metres apart when I noticed a tug about half mile ahead was beginning to cross the course with what looked like a fishing boat following a very long way behind at the same speed. I suspected that the fishing boat was under tow so altered course to take the longer route behind it. The others were oblivious to what appeared to be happening ahead and maintained their course directly towards the midpoint between the two vessels. A few minutes later the tow rope lifted momentarily from the surface of the sea and then dropped back giving John Derbyshire and Ian Godfrey who were by then almost on it such a fright that they both capsized, much to the amusement of the rest of the fleet.

It was a windy week and Peter Gale from Australia won the Open Championship leaving Geoff Woollen and myself to fight it out for the British title. This was decided in a close final race with Geoff eventually winning the British title and I was runner-up. Ian Godfrey, John Derbyshire and Trevor Gore also had their moments and ended up fourth, fifth and sixth respectively. The 1980 Championships at Parkstone Yacht Club was a three-way battle which Ian Godfrey eventually won from John Derbyshire and myself – the lesson for me from this championship – check everything before the racing starts – I had done this, except the stainless steel plate that connected the kicking strap to the mast and it was this that sheered.

At the beginning of 1981 we moved from Ladbroke Grove to Falmouth and while this made a perfect sailing ground it compounded the effort of getting to open meetings and training with other OKs. The nearest good OKs were at Parkstone, then a four and half hour drive on a good day. My results at the championships throughout the 1980s remained very consistent, always in the top six so the big distances I had to travel didn't impede me too much.

Clockwise from top left: Reaching in
Force 6 in 1877 (a Rowsell hull) at
the 1982 Nationals • In light winds
at Parkstone in 1980 • Running
alongside Dave Pinner at the 1984
Nationals at Royal Norfolk and
Suffolk YC

Top: Captain Khalid Akhtar of Pakistan being awarded the gold medal for the 1982 Asian Games, sailed in OKs. Earlier in the year he had been in the UK warming up at the Whitstable Nationals and went to Falmouth for some speed training with Henry. Pakistan were so pleased that he won that they celebrated by printing a stamp of Khalid.
Bottom: Event banner for the 1983 World Championship in Torbay

OK WORLDS '83
ROYAL TORBAY YACHT CLUB ENGLAND 22–30 JULY 1983

In the early 1980s Trevor Gore came into ascendency winning in 1982, and then taking four in a row from 1984, to 1987, while Alastair McMichael won in 1981 and 1983. Trevor Gore's last title was 1987 in Brixham, where he won from David Rose and myself. David Rose won in 1988 and 1990, with John Derbyshire, by then the RYA's Olympic manager, winning in 1989. Hedley Fletcher, who had been knocking on the door for some time, then won six in a row from 1991 to 1996.

The 1988 Championships at Eastbourne sticks in my mind for two reasons; landing in an on-shore breeze required one to sail fast into the waiting shore party who would then lift the boat with helm out of the sea. The second race was protested out as the finish line pin end mark had drifted to the extent that it was a hook finish. The race was initially thrown out then a counter protest caused it to be reinstated after which there was a further protest when it was finally thrown out at about 11 pm.

Although the brief for this article is to write about the UK OK fleet history I will write briefly on the international scene, but you will have to wait for next anniversary book to read my full recollections of OK Worlds.

Torbay 1983

THE 1983 WORLDS hosted by Royal Torbay Yacht Club received major support from a then national company C&A. Jonty Sherwill, Maureen and myself led the organisation from the OK Association together with Mick Bettesworth from the RTYC while Don and Brenda Andrews

The UK Team at the 1985 World Championship in Medemblik. L–R: back row: Rodney Tidd, Charles Dearlove, Henry Metcalfe, Simon Deeks, Alan Atkin, Jonty Sherwill, Trevor Gore; front row: Chris Starling, Nigel McKrill, Andy Williams and Tim O'Leary.

organised the British Open Championships. The final day of the British Championships raised hopes for a good blow in the worlds as it was blowing a good Force 5 easterly, which brings big waves into Torbay. The day was exciting until my boom broke and I had to limp home. However, this proved to be the 'last hurrah' from the wind gods' as the worlds were run in frustratingly little wind and much sitting around waiting for wind; good for holiday makers but not so good for sailors.

The Winner of the British Open Championship was Glen Collings from Australia while runner-up Alastair McMichael won the British title. The Worlds were won by Leith Armit from Stig Westergaard and Trevor Gore.

The 1989 Nationals and Worlds were held at Weymouth and the UK Organising team was led by Peter McIntyre. In the months leading up to the event, training was held every other weekend at Weymouth except when it clashed with an open meeting. The UK team had never been so prepared as it was for this event and like the Worlds at Torbay competition for places was intense particularly as a longstanding rule that entrants for World Championships were limited to 80 plus the winner of the previous worlds if they entered. This had the effect of ensuring the best possible teams from each nation. The racing in the middle of Weymouth Bay was pretty good as I remember until the penultimate day when for some reason only known to himself the race officer decided to set the windward mark right up against the cliffs in the north of the bay. This turned the final 200 meters of each windward leg into a complete lottery as the wind swooped down the high cliffs with no indication of where it was going to go or what direction. Everyone shot up and down in this game of snakes and ladders some changing 50 places in a couple of minutes. Despite protestations that evening, the same thing happened the next day, which put a bit of a dampener on the end of what had been a really good championship.

I was voted in as International President from 1985 and held this office for five years. This was particularly memorable for two unrelated events. Early on the West Germans came to me with a great deal of secrecy and asked for funding to make greater contact with the East German OK sailors. We knew there were significant numbers of OKs in East Germany but had virtually no contact with them. There had been increasing contact with Polish OK sailors and Poland on occasion sent sailors to some international events. The initiative was agreed and it was also agreed not to publicise it as the reaction of the authorities in East Germany was unpredictable. Looking back this small initiative was part of an 'organic' movement by many diverse sport, arts and other organisations to make greater contact and eventually contributed to the fall of the Berlin wall and the reunification of Germany.

The other event was when I was invited to speak first at the harbour side opening ceremony for the 1987 World Championships at Lulea. To my surprise and horror, the microphone was connected to not just nearest speakers around us but to a string of speakers half a mile around the harbour. The delayed echo of about three seconds meant I had to speak very slowly. However, I quickly got used to this echo but got bored and stopped my speech about half way through. The event sponsor and

Mayor of Lulea seemed pleased with the effectiveness of their speakers and my speech and so all was well in the end.

By 1990 the novelty of returning to Cornwall in the early hours of Monday morning and snatching a few hours sleep before getting up for work had well and truly worn off especially as we had two small children. I went to the Nationals at Highcliffe that year and managed to come sixth overall despite having no boat for boat practise. David Rose won that event from Hedley Fletcher and Gavin Waldron.

The following year I was better prepared having won Deben Week before going to the Nationals at Blackpool. I had good speed and in the first race after a mediocre start had worked my way up to fourth and had the leading boat in sight. I gybed and was immobilised with an enormous pain in my torso. I had cracked several ribs, the result of which was that it was all I could do to sit on the side of the cockpit. Even pulling slightly on the tiller was immensely painful. I could hardly talk and even getting into a RIB that showed up after five minutes, was agony. My boat was brought ashore in one piece and as the tide was out (and it goes out a long way at Blackpool), I was put on a tractor and taken up the beach and put in an ambulance and taken to Blackpool A&E.

Still, one OK helm's misfortune is another's fortune. A couple of helms had broken their masts and were making offers for my mast as I was taken up the beach as it was obvious I would not be using it again that week. As I proceeded slowly up the beach on the back of the tractor, a bidding war was going on around it. Eventually Ken Carroll won the auction. He offered to replace the mast with a new mast after the event but the clincher to the deal had been all the beer I could drink for the rest of the week. He knew something though as I was so dosed up on a cocktail of painkillers that I couldn't touch a drop for the whole week.

Although I was sailing again a few months later I didn't race OKs again until Brightlingsea Nationals in 1993 and wasn't on the pace. I reluctantly sold my last OK five years later. The next time I raced an OK was at the 50th anniversary when I borrowed a boat with a carbon mast. What a revelation – it was such a nice rig. Nowadays I still sail competitively in a B14 at Restronguet Sailing Club but as it's a two person boat the sitting out is much easier.

➤ ➤ ➤

PART 3
Tall Tales

Le Grand Tour – Mark Jackson

DEFINITION – NOUN – "A cultural tour of Europe formerly undertaken, especially in the 18th Century, by a young man of the upper classes as part of his education."

The grand tour was the traditional trip undertaken mainly by upper class European young men of sufficient means and rank (or those of more humble origin who could find a sponsor) when they had come of age (about the age of 21 years old).

This story recounts the adventures of young Australian and New Zealand OK Dinghy sailors who embarked on the ritual of the Grand Tour of Europe. During the 1970s and through the 1980s young sailors were attracted to the OK Dinghy class in Australia and New Zealand due to the depth of sailing talent, the opportunity to sail the boat of their idols (usually not much older than them), importantly for the social aspects offered by the class and also the chance to travel to Europe and continue the tradition of the Grand Tour.

In 1985, four young Australians aged 19 and 25, embarked on one such Grand Tour, meeting along the journey a young New Zealander filled with the same sense of adventure. Literary protocol, and laws of libel, dictate that names and identities be altered so as to protect the reputations of those involved, however in this case, reputations are well known and may in fact be enhanced by the story to follow.

1984 – THE PRE TOUR

THE STORY BEGINS a year earlier in 1984 when I decided to travel to Denmark for the OK Dinghy Worlds in Sønderborg. Travelling initially with Mark Fisher and Anthony Reynolds, flying into Frankfurt Airport, and after Mark Fisher handed over several thousand Deustche Marks to the local pickpockets and telling the police how it happened, we grabbed the hire car, retrieved our Needlespar masts from the freight desk, visited Mark's host family and finally headed north to Rudy Hitz's farm near Hamburg, where the famous 'Veal Sorrentino' had been stored for the winter. In Sønderborg we met up with Glenn Collings, Brent Williams, Kiwis Mark Wilcox (Tadpole, younger brother of Turtle) and Mark Crossen (aka Noddy) We also had the pleasure of staying with Nils Troland at his family home in Sønderborg.

The purpose of the 1984 trip was to undertake some early reconnaissance in preparation for the Grand Tour to be undertaken the following year. Previous Grand Tours in 1981 (Hyeres) involving Peter Jackson (Chocko), Peter Gale, Mark Fisher, Greg Wilcox (Turtle) and others, followed by 1983 (Torbay) again involving Chocko, Andre Blasse, Anthony Reynolds, Fisher and Turtle had established the basic idea of the Grand Tour. For young Australians and New Zealanders it inevitably included a visit to the mother country, or London at least, so following the worlds in Sønderborg where, by the way Glenn won and the other Aussies performed very well, it was a quick trip to London to pay respects to the country of my great grandparents. From London, it was back to Frankfurt to meet up Brent and Glenn for a quick drive in their old Opel sedan to Medemblik, Holland to check out the venue for the 1985 Worlds.

One final twist in the reconnaissance trip of 1984 was trying to get back to Germany from Holland in the days of European borders in an unregistered, uninsured German car. In the first attempt the German border guards refused us entry to Germany, so on being turned away, the Dutch on the other side, in between rolling around laughing, advised us to wait for 8 pm when the small border crossing 20 km further north is only staffed by the Germans until 8 pm. So successfully crossing back into Germany, Brent and I negotiated the sale of the unregistered Opel to the car wrecker before flying out of Frankfurt to commence the preparations for the Grand Tour the following year.

1985 – THE TOUR BEGINS

EARLY JUNE, ROGER Blasse, Peter Milne, Neil Williamson and myself have finished all the going away parties and fundraisers for our Grand Tour of Europe and leave Melbourne on a flight for Paris where Roger had organised a three-month hire of a brand new Renault 4. Arriving in Paris at 6 am on a Saturday morning, the French decided to enjoy their favourite pastime and the baggage handlers went on strike!.Vive le grève! So we waited at the airport long enough for the strike to be resolved and long enough for our hire car pick up in central Paris to close at midday. There are worse things to put up with. Two nights in Paris at the start of the Grand Tour, including running through the Louvre half an hour before closing to see the Mona Lisa. Tick, we've done the Louvre. C'était manifique!

Bright and early Monday morning we found our way to the car hire pick up, to be presented with a brand new Renault 4 with 9 km on the clock. We get the tow bar fitted and the car hire agent advised us that we won't fit all of our gear in the car. Oh non non, c'est possible. Pas problem. Well it fitted, but in the process of forcing the boot shut, we bent the brackets and left a 10 cm gap on both sides of the boot. We apologised, hoped it didn't rain and jumped in to drive north to Hamburg. As I was the only one of the four with previous experience in driving on the right hand side of the road with a left hand drive car, I was nominated driver. My instructions to the others in the car were simply to watch and don't panic. I proceeded to put down the window, put my arm out and with one hand on the horn and the other directing Paris traffic, we negotiated our way around the Arc de Triumphe and onto the motorway. Loaded down with gear we wound the little Renault up to 180 kph and our Grand Tour had finally commenced.

Next stop Hamburg and catch up with Reemt Reemtsma, who was living at the sailing club and we stayed at his mother's place nearby. Roger had shipped his boat and our masts, so we picked up his boat from the docks and then proceeded to gather the remaining three boats located in garages around northern Germany and southern Denmark. A quick practice sail in Sønderborg, with a spectacular capsize returning to the harbour and it was off to Kieler Woche, via the sporting goods store to buy extra sailing gear to recover from the shock of sailing in Northern Europe in June. The first regatta in Europe was a great eye opener to four young OK Dinghy sailors from Australia and a great start to the sailing part of the Grand Tour. Next stop, Medemblik, Holland.

Dutch Nationals and Worlds

TRANSPORT WAS ARRANGED with fellow sailors and towing Roger's double trailer behind the Renault we headed for Holland. We had organised to stay at the world famous Brakeboer as part of the reconnaissance the year before and we presented ourselves to our host Jack. Jack regaled us with stories of his travelling around and across Australia as a young man in a Ford Falcon Holden (humorous only to older Australians). The Dutch Nationals were uneventful for me spending several days at the physiotherapist with a torn meniscus cartilage, not to mention the infamous incident with Peter Milne and the stolen German beer glasses from Kiel when Peter sliced open his foot on a broken glass left carelessly on the ground between the boats. Needless to say Peter couldn't sail the nationals or the worlds and had to be content enjoying the social aspects of Medemblik.

The most memorable evening in Medemblik was catching up with the locals at the Nightclub, 'Black and White' or better remembered by another name. The club lived up to its name and reputation and the locals called in for a visit and started an all in fight, which ended with the Aussies and Kiwis running back to the Brakeboer and the protection of Jack, who proceeded to pull his baseball bat out from behind the bar and go after the thugs. We licked our wounds, had a few more beers and reported the events to the police the following day. Unfortunately our little Renault was not so lucky. With French tourist number plates, the locals took their anger out on the little car and kicked in most of the panels. Our trusty Renault was looking decidedly worse for wear after only one month.

NORDIC CHAMPIONSHIPS DENMARK

THE WORLDS CONCLUDED, trophies presented, final beers and farewell to Jack and we packed up the boats and headed for Ishoj, near Copenhagen for the Nordic Championships and the first appearance of the trusty two-man tents packed in the container in Australia. This was to be the new accommodation standard for the next six weeks. From the Nordics, Peter Milne left the Grand Tourists to finally get some sailing at the British Nationals and headed off with Bjørn Westergaard and some Danes for Old Blighty. A young New Zealander, Nigel Soper, had escaped the instruction of the newly crowned world champion, Leith Armit, and accepted the vacated fourth seat in the Renault.

SAILING FINISHED – TOUR CONTINUES

LEAVING DENMARK FOR Hamburg to drop off boats to return to Australia, the Grand Tour headed south. Frankfurt, Heidelberg, Tried to see the shroud of Jesus and the manufacture of floor vinyl and off to Munich. There were two things in Munich; beer and rain. The

Hofbräuhaus proved to be a good escape from the rain in the camping park, but after being soaked through in our little two man tents, we vowed the next night was a hotel. Out of Germany and into Austria and a nice little guest house in central Innsbruck. Very nice Weiner Schnitzel and several beers made a very pleasant two-night stay.

At this stage of the tour we were on a schedule to meet up with Frank Schoenfeld at the Pirat European Championships commencing a couple of days later in Interlaken Switzerland. Through Lichten-stein and into Switzerland, we found Frank and enjoyed a Pirat party complete with Apple Schnapps, which proved to be a mistake for our finely tuned beer adjusted stomachs. Leaving Frank to continue with the Pirats, the journey continued through Switzerland, visiting the Jungfrau, Eiger, took a ride on the cable car and finally settled in the Zermatt camping park to take in some mountain air in the shadow of the Matterhorn.

Zermatt proved very appealing and we stayed longer than expected. Mountain walks to the cafes and bars up the mountain were a sight with Aussies and New Zealanders in the mountains in shorts, T-shirts and jandles (thongs/ flip flops). Neil Williamson also managed a day of gla-cier skiing on the slopes of the Matterhorn.

After a few days relaxing, it was off to find a beach, so back into the Renault and over the mountain passes, which by this stage were taken in first gear, into Italy, out of Italy and onto the French Riviera. It didn't take us long to work out that the OK Dinghy Grand Tour did not include Monte Carlo. Our little Renault and two man tents were not very welcome, so we headed west past Marseille and found a huge camp-ing ground half empty except for German tourists, right on the beach. We enjoyed a week in the sun, drinking cheap local wine and eating baguettes, fromage and moules.

Back into the Renault and off to La Rochelle, then north to St Malo, Mont St Michel and Cherbourg for a ferry to England. We drove off the ferry and had a look around Portsmouth and Southampton, a quick trip to Cowes on the Isle of Wight and off to London where we able to meet up again with Tadpole and Noddy, still in Europe 12 months later. We found the unregistered 'doss house' with mattresses on the floor, one bathroom and no shower for 20 boarders. We truly felt we were follow-ing the noble tradition of the Grand Tour.

After a couple of weeks in London and driving about the countryside in a left hand drive car, the Renault needed to return to Paris as we were at the end of our three month hire period. Roger volunteered to take the car back and try to explain how a three-month-old car was now a wreck running on two cylinders and every panel dented. According to Roger, he dropped it off and left while there was a lot of looking and wondering what happened to what was a brand-new Renault 4 three months earlier. The little car had served us well.

Meanwhile back in London, our Grand Tour was coming to an end. I was flying out of Amsterdam, so a train, ferry and bus to Amsterdam saw me dropped at Central Station and booking into a share cabin of a 'Boatel' moored behind the station for a night. The following day, wandering down the main street, I bumped into Peter Milne who had just arrived from Copenhagen and was catching the same flight out back to Australia that evening. Spending a pleasant day, declining the offers of drugs and prostitutes, we visited the museums and art galleries, caught up on what had happened in the previous six weeks and then completed our cultural tour through Europe.

We had joined a club of young Australians and New Zealanders who had undertaken the Grand Tour. While our tour followed the tradition of sailing events and visiting new and different places, each of the OK Dinghy Grand Tours before and following 1985 was unique and based on the goals and personalities of the sailors on tour. Each tour has its own great stories and memories for those who participated and these stories continue to be shared today when we all catch up for another OK Dinghy event. The Grand Tour was a right of passage for many of us and hopefully many reading this will have fond memories of your their OK Dinghy journey through Europe.

I did it my way – Jörg Rademacher

Jörg Rademacher gets lost at the 2006 Belgian Championship

AFTER MANY SAILORS FROM THE Haltern OK Dinghy team raved about the Belgian championship in Antwerp, I decided to join them in 2006. Since Ralf Mackmann wanted to arrive with a complete family and caravan, we had thrown his boat on my trailer on Friday and set off on Saturday morning, with Tommy Neveling and Klaus Stephan, two more OK Dinghy sailors from Haltern. After a traffic jam and a wrong turn in Antwerp it was already really tight. Just 15 minutes before the start of the race, I drove into the sailing club grounds and Ralf was delighted that he could finally put his boat together. The

Belgians, however, were nice enough to postpone the start a bit and after an alarming rig-up we managed it just in time.

In light winds, three races were sailed on the small lake Galgenweel next to the river Schelde and the centre of Antwerp. All the races were sailed in light winds and were won by Ralf 'the executor'.

After the races I was really thirsty and I literally ran to my car to get some beer. In my hurry I left the keys in the car. Of course all the car doors were locked, but Michel Lesure cracked the car in record time with a wire coat hanger. So I thought that was the 'faux pas' for the weekend, but as it turned out later, this was not the last to come.

The organisers then offered an extensive buffet and so we had a good lunch with beer and wine at the end of a nice sailing day.

Later, the Belgians invited us to an eel party at another sailing club. This was, of course, a compulsory event for me and after a short drive we drank some beers at the new location. At some point, after a little peeing, I spontaneously decided to go home, without telling our Belgian hosts.

I walked on foot. As it turned out later, the path was right in front of me, which is easy to walk in 30 minutes. But sadly, I started a phase of 'uncontrolled action'.

After finding some self-control again, it was already too late: I fell to my chest in a muddy bog hole, and the area around me did not look at Antwerp at all. I had the feeling I was in the dark woods from the Twin Peaks series.

'Keep a stiff upper lip,' I thought by myself. I freed myself from the muddy hole and ran off. At some point I would have to return to an inhabited area where I could grab a taxi. Instead, it became more and more unreal and I paved my way through reeds and other morasses. Fences did not stop me, and for a long time and I was on my way through the Belgian wilderness.

Suddenly I found myself on the site of a petroleum refinery. All around me hissed and fizzled the piping and valves, but there were no people to be seen anywhere. I briefly played with the idea of turning the valves a little to force an encounter with potential taxis, but I decided against it. Karsten Hitz commented later, that when deciding the other way, the Belgian press would probably have adopted it, so I should not have written this report myself.

After I had overcome more fences, I left the plant again and so slowly I worried about the start for the last races. After all sorts of reeds, mats and fences, I passed a farm at 6:00 am at sunrise. I let my eyes wander over my outfit and dismissed the plan to ring the peasants from their bed. Instead I laid down for a little nap on a straw ball. I had wandered all night, climbed over fences and so I was dog-tired.

At about 7:00 am a rain shower awakened me and I continued my journey. After 30 minutes I actually came to a small suburb. I looked at a pub, which had not opened, but the staff were already behind the counter. Since I looked like a bog man they did not open to me, but were so kind to call me a taxi.

The taxi driver was also not immediately ready to take me with him, but when I gave him the seriousness of the situation, he let me in. On the 10-minute journey I described to him the events of the night and he did not stop laughing.

Once back at the lake I ran past Klaus Stephan, who looked at me with astonishment and wonder. Without further explanation, I went

straight to my car. There I had fortunately already built my bunk and so I called it a day.

I planned to take it a little calmer the next year and take a GPS device.

Memorable for all the wrong reasons – Jan Tyler

OUR FAMILY'S TRIP TO ADELAIDE in 1974 for the National and World Championships was memorable to me – for all the wrong reasons.

The drive took three days across the middle of a very hot Australia from Sydney to Adelaide in summer and for our two daughters, Karyn four and a half years old and Leanne 18 months old, that was a long time. But as young parents, Bill and I managed – somehow. But that was the easy part.

On arrival, our booking in hostel-type accommodation had fallen through and we ended up in an empty caravan on West Beach. Of course we hadn't taken any linen, and cooking utensils, plates and cutlery were sparse. Fortunately the local Adelaide sailing ladies helped out and lent us supplies.

That first night, Karyn wasn't well and we discovered she had chicken pox. Oh joy! We went through quite a lot of calamine lotion trying to ease the itch and discomfort. Leanne waited to get the chicken pox until the start of our journey home two weeks later.

In the middle of all this, our washing was stolen from the local Laundromat. Foolishly I left it for a short while and returned to our caravan. When I returned the machine was empty. At first I thought I was looking in the wrong machine, but no, I found out that it wasn't the first time this had happened. It wasn't much consolation to me at the time.

Surprisingly, all this didn't deter us and over the years we continued

to travel to many more regattas and championships, until 2014. Forty years of great times and wonderful experiences with the OK family.

Performance of the Year I

During the 1990s the British newsletter carried many tales of derring-do. Here's the first from 1994.

THE PERFORMANCE OF THE YEAR is not concerned with what goes on whilst racing, that follows a predictable pattern. What we are concerned with is original, imaginative and sometimes spontaneous, sometimes carefully planned acts that take place before and after the formalities of the day's racing.

The trail started in New Zealand and a good start it was, with attempted immolation, destruction of crown property and what in the UK would have put the SAS on standby.

Britain's Alistair Deaves played a risky game by doing his turn early in the morning – his audience nearly missed it. There were two parts to this attempt at immortality. Firstly he decides to wash all his money, airline ticket home and passport in the campsite washing machine. OK, so far not all that original. What happened next was an incredible display. The fact that he didn't need his passport for a few weeks did not, thankfully, diminish his burning desire to prove what a practical, resourceful in an emergency type he is. He spies the gas burner, congratulates himself on yet another display of Deaves' initiative, lights the thing whilst still thinking what a clever old thing he really is, holds the damp passport over the flame and watches as it incinerates – quite wonderful.

By the end of January, Martin Jaggs and Stuart Sykes decide it's time to strike. They chose their moment well to cause maximum embarrassment to Brenda [Andrews] and maximum inconvenience to Norbert [Petraucsh] and his wife. Briefly what they do is hijack Napier Airport on the morning that the four mentioned are due to leave (Jaggs and Sykes fresh from the prizegiving). They insist on checking everyone in, weighing their luggage and then labelling it. At this point Stuart sees his chance. Norbert, he notices, is going to Auckland, so the only thing to do is send his and his wife's belongings to Wellington. After a quick ride on the luggage conveyor belt off they go to check the airplane and chat to the pilot about flying them home – very good effort – original and lots of inconvenience for everyone around them (especially Norbert).

Next to Holland. The whole British contingent should be congratulated on the magnificent singing. Well, it got lots of applause. The barman also deserves a mention for the free rounds that he kept supplying. Individual mentions must go to John Atkinson for a great display of gluttony. Howard Atkin for being stripped naked and also for arranging to start his new job on the Tuesday and finding out once he got to Holland that his ferry home wasn't until Tuesday. Final mention must go to Giles Hudson. After a standard walk back to the campsite from the bar – rugby tackling each other, a bit of landscape gardening, our man Hudson demonstrates to the assembled few his dyke jumping technique. Vertically he got it spot on, horizontally, sadly lacking.

At the Europeans, the combined British and Danish teams performed fantastically by being threatened with expulsion before the event even began by engaging in a food and firehose fight in the dining tent, a very good start and helped set the tone for the event.

Personally I think that all the above events pale into insignificance compared with the final one I describe which is undoubtedly performance of the year. The day Alan Atkin set his beard alight. Early in the year, the Atkins decide to have a quiet, family night in – Mum, Dad and the kids. After dinner, they settle down, Alan decided he could do with a drink and thought that a flaming Drambuie would go down just great. I'm sure you can guess the rest. Apparently, Alan had let it burn for too long, so it got too hot. In this situation, it appeared there was only one thing to do. Instead of drinking it, pour it all over your face.

Methodical Approach

Victorian Peter Gale became the first Australian to win the OK Dinghy World Championship. at Hyeres, France, in July 1981.

AUSTRALIAN SAILING 1981 – I ended up with an OK because it seemed the strongest local single-handed class, and the Worlds were on in New Zealand. My first OK was old and heavy. I kept it only for one month, then sold it and bought a new one. With that boat I finished fourth in my first Nationals in Christmas 1976. I was wrapt. because I didn't expect to go that well. In the Worlds in New Zealand I finished 22nd. In 77-78 I went to the Nationals in Hobart. I had problems with my new boat so I borrowed a boat which fell to bits, basically because I was pretty slack. I finished seventh overall. After that I went to the Finn

Nationals at Lake Macquarie. I won the invitation race and one heat and I had two seconds, but I was competitive only in the light races. I decided to leave Finn sailing to the big boys. Mainly I went just to get experience.

In 1978 I sailed in Kiel Week in Germany in the OK. I finished halfway through the fleet. For the first time in my sailing career I was starting to adopt a methodical approach, probably because in the Hobart Nationals I had some good places but lost a good overall position because of bad preparation.

In 78-79 I went to the Adelaide Nationals and won the first two races. Then I started to go downhill. I think my problem was that I didn't know how to win; I ended-up second to Bruce Ashton. I just didn't sail as well as he did. I sailed very poorly in light weather, unusual for me, and I started to think I had a problem. I didn't believe I could win.

I went to Brisbane in 78-79 for the Finn Nationals again, In a borrowed boat I had a couple of good heat placings but I was no good in a blow and I finished ninth. Basically I wanted to reassure myself that I couldn't sail a Finn. I just wasn't competitive in heavy weather.

[For the 1979 Worlds] I got assistance from the Victorian OK Dinghy Association to go to Norway. For a change I tried to experiment with the sail and mast and I did a lot of physical training. I went and Terry Bellair, who makes a lot of the OK sails in Australia, and we sailed chartered boats. I was running 11th but I got disqualified for an early start. They ran out of wind and it was a five-race series so they had to count all the races. Because I had to count a disqualification I ended up 29th. After the Worlds in Norway I went to England. The English boats had finished third, fifth and seventh in the Worlds so I decided I'd like to sail in the English Nationals, which I won easily. I had four firsts, a second and a third.

It was pretty good to win, it was a sort of hurdle, getting it out of the way, actually winning a big series. After the English Nationals I went to Denmark and sailed at the same club as Paul Kirketerp, the '75 and '76 OK World Champion.

I came home and won the Nationals in Brisbane. I was pretty happy about that. It seemed like it was no longer a problem for me to actually lead a series. That meant I was assisted by the Victorian OK Association and the VYC to go to the OK Worlds in Sweden in the winter of 1980 at Varberg. I organised a borrowed boat myself for that series, and ended up sixth. By this time I wasn't so uneasy about sailing against 80 others.

I think I was becoming much more methodical. I started to think analytically about what I was doing and the way I was doing things. I

Left: Peter Gale after winning in Hyeres
Right: Australian Championship 1981
Below: Adelaide 1978

was also thinking a lot more about the racing. After the British Nationals in 1979 I went to the Finn Gold Cup as a spectator and I was fortunate to go out on a boat and help the German coach. I was really amazed by the way they approached a campaign, and it confirmed that I was starting to really do it properly.

I was reasonably happy after Sweden. It was the best an Australian had ever done in Europe. In the meantime the overall Australian standard was improving. A lot of boats in Melbourne were going well.

[In the next Nationals] Peter Takle won them easily. I was second. Peter sailed a better series and was better prepared than I, or anybody else. He managed almost a 'leapfrog' development in boatspeed. After that I decided I had to try to improve my performance in heavy weather. I started using a much softer mast and a fuller sail, looking for a more versatile rig, I think.

We had the Interdominion at Mordialloc at Easter and I won that, with Peter Takle second. I felt pretty happy about winning the Interdominion, as I knew the local guys were going pretty well. I figured the Australian team could do well in the Worlds and there was a chance for an Australian to win. Before I went to Europe, I did a lot of sailing off Chelsea by myself. I started to run daily and I was swimming a bit. I felt I was a lot better prepared, and I had my own boat for the first time. I was so much more experienced than I had been before. It's a thing you have to learn – how to win a series. When you're in front in a series, knowing how to handle it can be a real problem. I'm not saying I have mastered it either, but I'm a lot closer than I have been. I still worry.

The first thing we got to over there was Kiel Week. The series was cut to five races due to lack of winds, and I stuffed it. I had two firsts and two seconds. On one of the firsts I was disqualified for an early start, so that was taken away from me, and the other race I didn't finish was a really light day when I fell off the side of the boat going downwind. I tipped over and sank slowly into the Baltic. Everybody sailed past laughing. I ended up nowhere. Peter Takle came third. However at Kiel Week I sailed well enough to finish at the top of the fleet, and I figured after that if I didn't screw up I could probably do okay in France.

[At the 1981 Worlds] I won the invitation race but I received a caution for Rule 60, Means of Propulsion. They didn't throw me out, they just gave me a warning. That was probably pretty good. Then I won the first heat of the Worlds sailed in about 10 knots of breeze. But the next day there were two races. In the first I was disqualified for an early start, and in the afternoon race I came 18th. Then I thought I'd stuffed it again. At that stage things weren't going too well. The next day, in heat four, I came seventh. Then in heat five I came second, again in a light to medium breeze. I came back to shore and was amazed to see I was second overall, as everybody else had been really inconsistent. I was .3 of a point behind a Swedish guy. That lifted my spirits. I was sort of surprised that I was back in it.

For heat six I figured all I had to do was have a good solid finish to put me in a pretty good position. I finished sixth and I sailed pretty conservatively. I sailed up the works on the same side as the Swedish guy leading the series, even though he was well behind in that heat. After the race I was 11.7 points up, and leading the series. I figured I was pretty safe, but I still wasn't really confident. In heat seven the wind shifted 180 degrees, and they stopped it halfway through. That meant I had won the Worlds.

I think relief was the biggest feeling. I didn't really think about it until a day or two afterward, and I was pretty happy about it then.

[Sailing the OK] is pretty hard physically, and there's a fair bit of pain involved. I've really enjoyed going overseas, but the build-up to the Worlds wasn't a deliberate approach when I first got into the class. When you play fullback you don't even think about kicking a goal. That is until you run past centre and think, maybe I will.

British Nationals, Plymouth 1979 – Richard Morell

IT WAS THE WEEK AFTER the Fastnet race disaster. Rodney's camper van was struggling to tow the 'Triple decker' trailer up the hills because the exhaust pipe was blowing. The triple decker trailer was a contraption that Rodney built on a friend's car transporter road trailer. It consisted of four up right metal poles and lots of rope to tension the structure. The three OK Dinghies were carried one above the other supported by slings from the uprights. The whole rig was tensioned by the winch that used to pull cars on. It did sway about a bit, but to Rodney's credit it did work.

So the ever-resourceful Rodney pulled over to the side of the road to repair the offending hole with an exhaust repair Gumgum bandage, a coke can and all held together with the use of a wire coat hanger.

We made it to the Mayflower Sailing Club in Plymouth where Rodney parked his motor home at the top of the slipway and announced to anyone who would listen that he had broken down and it couldn't be moved. There was a strict no cars in the dinghy park policy, but Rodney managed to get around that. Pole position. Some kind person had left a Laser dinghy alongside Rodney's motor home. I'd never really been sure what these 'iron boards' had been built for but in a flash of brilliance we realised that they are in fact portable sinks. So each morning after a fry up the cockpit bung would go in, we'd boil the kettle and fill the cockpit with hot soapy water. The deck space is ideal for drying the dishes. I think one morning we over did it with the 'fairy liquid' as there were complaints of bubbles blowing everywhere in the blustery conditions.

On one day the conditions were so rough outside Plymouth Sound that they had to call the fleet back in to the Sound because the organisers were having trouble controlling the rescue boats.

Does anyone remember the race when the Navy decided to tow one of its large ships; yes we had a few then, through the fleet? The people who got through in time had a huge advantage and the rest had to wait for it to pass. One intrepid sailor, who shall remain nameless, tried to sail between the ship and the tugboat not realising there was a fixed link between the two at water level. Fortunately he bit the dust before he got that far. There was a lot of talking about it afterwards.

There was another day when the fair weather sailors decided that a Radio 1 roadshow near the sailing club was more attractive than going out in windy conditions.

Ian Godfrey was National Champion, and Peter Gale from Australia was the open Champion.

I accidentally poured beer on Johnny McIntyre during the whale dance and then realised that it wasn't a clever thing to do. Fortunately he was OK about it. Johnny had a smart Escort Mexico with large lights on the front.

On Saturday morning, after a week's rest, Rodney's motorhome had recuperated enough to get us back to Burton-on-Trent, or so I thought…

The motorhome broke down in Walsall (in the Midlands) and we spent hours in the back finishing off the beer. As in we, I don't mean Rodney because he was still in charge of the motorhome that wasn't going anywhere. When the recovery driver finally arrived he asked Rodney where he wanted the motorhome taking. For some strange reason we ended up at Jeremy's house.

This must have been a bit of a shock for Jeremy Wicks when he woke up the next morning to see Rodney's motor home and a triple OK trailer parked on his drive. Rodney was probably greeted with the suitable abuse that only Jeremy can welcome people with. It's like a small Viking who has had far too many beers the night before, has a throbbing headache, and you've just trodden on his small toe in big boots. To make matters worse, when I stepped on to the rear end of the trailer, after it had been uncoupled, it promptly put a mast through one of Jeremy's garage windows, which as you can imagine didn't go down too well.

Teenage Ambitions – 1965

SOUTH AFRICA – ONE BIG disappointment I have as OK chairman and that is the lack of young 18-year-olds, etc getting into OKs. This is the craft for the teenager who has ambitions of being a Finn man later. All members of our association should concentrate on encouraging this age group in OKs. The low costs of manufacture should also be an added incentive.

No OK home-built should cost more than R 130 to R 140, for the complete amateur putting in a couple of hours in the evening plus a Saturday or Sunday should be able to finish an OK in five to six weeks. It is up to members to let the youngsters know these facts. In Durban our OK chaps are only too pleased to get others to sail these sporting craft. We feel anyone who has not tried an OK is missing something

The Flag Scandal of Olpenitz – Thorsten Schmidt

IT WAS GERMANY IN 1970. We are in the middle of the cold war between the two supervisors, the US and the Soviet Union. The summer of love is just over and around the world the youth rebels against the prevailing social structures and the war in Vietnam. In Germany, too, demonstrations are on the agenda, student unrest, the APO (Extra-Parliamentary Opposition) and the founding of the RAF (Red Army Fraction terror group) determine the political events and want to get rid of the niff of the post-war period and the remnants of the Nazi period. In the sport of sailing, old men are governing the sailing federation (DSV) according to strict labels as in the times of the last German emperor.

But even before sailing, the social upheaval does not stop. For about five years, OK Dinghies have been sailing on rivers Alster and Elbe in Hamburg. Young, long-haired and unsuitable sailors sail regattas on this new, fast single-handed dinghy from Denmark, celebrate with wild parties and have unconstrained sympathy for communism and Viet Cong.

The core of the scene are the brothers Jungblut. Their father is a pilot on the river Elbe and they have grown close to the water in Hamburg-Övelgönne. Thomas Jungblut is one of the best German OK Dinghy sailors, along with his brothers Christian, Florian and Andreas. To be able to sail in a German regatta you have to be a member of a sailing club. Because they do not feel like the conservative structures in the sailing clubs, the brothers founded their own club with a few OK Dinghy friends on January 1, 1970, and used the flag of the Viet Cong as a template for the pennant.

This is apparently not the end of the provocation.

On May 1, the day of the workers' movement, the International Campaign of the Working Class and a holiday in Germany, an OK Dinghy Regatta took place on the Baltic Sea. The starting point on land is the NATO naval base Olpenitz. Florian Jungblut comes too late and misses the first race of the regatta. From boredom and arrogance, and on the NATO ground, on which the OK Dinghy sailors are guests, he hoists the flag of the USSR and the great scandal is perfect.

The OK Dinghy sailors are blocked by the national federation, cannot participate in Kiel Week, and even in the political newspapers of Germany it is reported about the alleged international incident by the revolting OK Dinghy sailors.

A year later, the excitement has been forgotten, and Thomas Jungblut becomes the first German OK world champion in 1971.

Since these times the OK Dinghy sailors in Germany have the reputation to be particularly wild, revolutionary and unadjusted.

Performance of the Year 2 – 1995

IT HAS COME TO THAT time of year again. The main events of the season are over and all that is left to do is to sit back and reflect on what we and others have done and to think how we arc going to improve our performance next time around.

Although the bar does tend to be the main focal point for performing, the real top boys are happy to oblige whilst in a completely sober state. This is good as it allows for performing throughout the day or at the one day opens. Hence we have Rodney Thorne actually screwing his boat to his road trailer whilst going from Waldringfield to Upper Thames. Then there was Rodney Thorne who tied a huge plastic bag filled with water, for his solar shower, to a television aerial screwed to the side of a caravan. Finally there was Rodney Thorne, who had meticulously planned his trip to Waldringfield for the Cartoon Trophy (I know as 1 spoke to him just once or twice in the week beforehand). He actually left Burton the afternoon of the day before it started. This is remarkable stuff, though the story regains its credibility when we learn that in a fit of enthusiasm he managed to forget his rudders. By the time he had turned around at Northampton and driven back home, he decided that perhaps leaving Saturday morning might be more realistic.

Enough of that, who have been the real big performers this year? The idea of self-inflicted injury seems to have been fashionable. We had David Carroll appearing at Hythe with a broken nose after a game of 'slugs' the previous night (don't ask what that entails).

He would suffer personal injury again, this time at Brightlingsea. A vindaloo in the early evening followed by a phal when the bar shut, led to extreme discomfort whilst on the water the next day. In fact, the situation got so severe that David was obliged to perform what can only be described as a 'Mark Fisher' from the side of his boat. This took place just seven minutes before the start. Unfortunately for David he lost marks for actually pulling his wetsuit down rather than leaving it in place.

A couple of weeks later was the Nationals for those of you who didn't bother, then you are most unfortunate. If you hear any stories about how good it was, they are not exaggerated. It was incredible. To give the full list of commendations would be far too long, and an abbreviated report will have to suffice. Perhaps first mention should go the batty old dear behind the bar. (I did actually ask her if she was mad and she said that she was.) She apologised for having no red wine on the first evening, so gave wine glasses full of port for 60p. Well it does look the same.

The prize-giving was the one to end all prizegivings. It had everything. It had Fletch dancing naked on a pool table. Laurie Evans necking decanters of rum and coke. Pete Waymouth drinking beer from a used potty, naked men dancing on the balcony. By the end of the evening Terry Curtis had given up trying to keep his clothes on.

With all these tails of daring exploits it may look like it was going to be a hard decision to decide on the actual performance of the year. It was not hard though. There can really be only one winner this year. The performance involved a high-speed car chase, the police, fire, danger, the lot. Last year Martin Jaggs hijacked Napier airport. This year he rode down the M6 on his new motorbike at 150 mph whilst his bag which contained his suit and shoes, on the back of his bike was on fire. Of course, no one could tell him, he was the fastest thing on the road. Eventually a Sierra Cosworth managed to pull alongside and pointed out the inferno just inches behind Jaggs' bum. Sensibly Jaggs stops and dumps the ashes. Off he goes again, upon reaching the roadworks on the motorway, he reduces his speed to 110 mph and drives along the closed lane when, not too surprisingly, the police stop him. A quick resume of Jaggs' day amuses the policeman so much that he let him off.

So if you watch the programmes on TV of police footage showing lunatic drivers and you see a flame going down the M6 at 150 mph, you'll know where you read about it first.

An English Affair – Rodney Thorne and Richard Morrell

ONE YEAR STUART GOODMAN OF Burton Sailing Club quali-fied for the OK Dinghy World Championships in the South of France. They decided to go down in Jeremy Wicks' company Ford Capri. It was blisteringly hot and the fair skinned Goodmans (Martin and Stu-art) soon turned into 'Lemmy the lobsters'. It was also at this event that Jeremy's car had a coming together with another car. If annoyed, the 'little fella' can get a bit grumpy. Most of the time he is fine and even better if you offer to buy him a beer. This accident annoyed him, and it got worse and worse. The guy who had driven into him came from England, which didn't impress him, but at least there wasn't a language barrier. What really annoyed him was that the guy came from Burton-on-Trent and he lived only a few miles from Jeremy. It was like, if you wanted to drive into me, you could have done it in Burton-on-Trent High Street, why did you have to drive all of the way to the South of France to drive into me? He had a point and it was amusing to hear the tale. Talking of Jeremy, he must be one of the only people who has rally driven his car at the bottom of Foremark Reservoir. Yes, this was when it was all dug out and before they pumped the water in. The weather was very dry, and there was a large cloud of muddy dust rising from deep down in the bottom of Foremark reservoir and out popped a 1.3GL Ford Escort, one careful owner.

Travelling to India

The 2003 OK Dinghy World Championship was held in Goa, India, the first time the class had opted for an 'exotic' location. Various problems including lack of information, changing the venue twice and general lack of confidence, meant that only one full container from Europe and one 20 footer from New Zealand made the trip for the lowest attended world championship ever. But in terms of organisation and shore side, it was perhaps one of the best championships ever. And it also produced the only Asian winner of the world title, Nitin Mongia, overcoming the favourite Nick Craig, who would have to wait another two years before he would win the first of his world crowns.

COMING DOWN THROUGH THE THIN lining of clouds and into the brilliance of the sunrise, India appeared on the view screen as the Emirates flight descended towards Mumbai. The air looked red with dust and sand, and you could almost smell the fragrance of Bombay drifting up through the atmosphere. It was quite tangible and yet, almost invisible through the haze of the early morning. It looked hot, dusty and dirty. And it was.

The war was on, but who cared? We were going to Goa. Nick was there as well making all his usual smells and noise. However, this time he excelled himself and the lady in the seat next to him on the flight out actually sprayed him with perfume while he was asleep to try to obliterate some of his body odour.

Trying to get through Mumbai immigration with an OK centreboard wrapped up in cardboard and a sail in a large box [carefully packed by Nick in the check-in queue at Heathrow Airport with the help of several other passengers – one of whom pulled a knife on Nick, only to help him cut the cardboard to the correct shape] was an experience in itself. Not only did they not really understand what we were carrying, but they then thought we would try and sell them and kept asking what they were worth. We eventually smooth talked our way through Mumbai Customs only to have an hour and a half wait for a coach connection to the domestic airport that lasted about 10 minutes.

On arrival in Goa we all waited on the hot plane while an even hotter bus arrived to drive us to the terminal building – about 30 metres away. It would have been quicker and cooler to walk it but we weren't allowed to.

And so, finally, to the sailing. A more idyllic venue for a sailing regatta would be hard to find. Picture the scene. A palm tree littered beach, lapping waves from the Indian Ocean, grassy gardens of a 5-star hotel, dinghy park on the beach. Come off the water after a hard day's sailing to be greeting by a military band, tea on the lawn, followed by beer and curry under the palm trees along the shore or in one of the many restaurants nearby.

The racing was characterised by winds off the sea with a strong tide, running on the left side of the course, out in the main channel of the river. There were frequent large shifts, generally favouring those who had banged corners – often opposite corners were favoured and those who sailed conservatively sometimes ended up down the drain. Occasionally it paid to play the shifts up the middle, but often those who were looking good and tacked to consolidate found they had lost out to a corner banger by an enormous margin. When the wind was up the sailing was fantastic.

The water temperature in the mid-20s meant you were never cold, even on the windiest days. All said, it was similar to sailing an open meeting. With only 25 boats, there was plenty of space to find clear lanes and you could generally sail your own race. The results reflected this and were fairly consistent over the week throughout the whole fleet. Short, square start lines, combined with very well laid courses and immaculate race management provided a model example of how to run a regatta. It would have been very interesting to see what would have happened in an 80-boat fleet.

Nitin Mongia's win was fairly decisive. He was sailing fast and seemed to know where the shifts were coming from. He was also the only sailor with a coach boat. His plan seemed to be to lead from the front and just cover those behind, often covering Nick tack for tack. Whether this would have worked in an 80-boat fleet is hard to judge but I suspect his win would not have been as decisive.

One of the event organisers was Major Gautama Dutta, an Indian OK sailor and sometime publicity officer of OKDIA. A soap opera of epic proportions had started back in December when Gautama has asked for a Laser to be included in the British/German/Swedish container, to be imported into India. Everyone assumed the paperwork would be in order, but that was far from the case. The lack of paperwork and Gautama's repeated insistence that everything was OK, meant that the container, containing the OKs and the Laser, were stuck in Mormagao Customs until half way through the Indian Nationals, the week before the worlds, with a couple of the sailors – Mary Reddyhoff and Hans Elkjær – spending a day in the agent's office arguing to have it released. By the end of the week Gautama had a new name.

Finally it was, but the saga continued until the 11th hour. On the final morning of the Worlds Nick and an increasingly murderously looking Rudiger Prinz had to take a fast boat ride with Gautama across the bay to the agent's office to secure the release of the Laser and the clearance for the rest of the gear and boats to return back to Europe without difficulty. In order to stop his nice new Laser returning from whence it came, Gautama finally handed over the duty while the sailors were in the process of loading the container for the return trip.

The prizegiving dinner, set on the lawns of another, rather posh, hotel, started with unlimited free alcohol and with Nitin and the Kiwis knocking back triple rum and cokes. The OKs then were encouraged to join in with the floorshow limbo dancing and the like – but generally ended up demolishing the set.

Eventually Gouch collapsed into a heap and got thrown into the pool. Then things really started to deteriorate into mayhem. Most of the Indian guests just watched bemused as virtually all the European and

Antipodean competitors ended up in the pool – even holding back the Indian bouncers – who were fairly small for the job it must be admitted – while the task was completed. After this they closed the free bars and everyone went into the upstairs bar all dripping wet. The bouncers followed and guarded the other guests against the rowdy sailors, literally standing in the middle of where everyone was dancing.

Nick was his usual self, drowning his sorrows in a never ending run on the bar. The evening turned into a bit of a blur and we finally left the hotel at 1 am. Eight of us got into Gautama's car and went back to our hotel, where Nick held an impromptu party. Gautama rang one of his officers to get a case of beer (it's now 1.30 am) while Nick phoned half the hotel at random, waking them up and asking them if they would like to come to his party. No one showed.

The beer was warm so I idled away the hours throwing Nick's clothes into the overhead fan and seeing where they ended up. Annoyingly he didn't have a hangover in the morning, although Gautama was making enquiries about who had rung his wife on his mobile phone at 2 in the morning.

The final day was spent doing some shopping in Panaji and taking in Anjuna Flea Market, which came complete with hoards of ageing hippies. A final curry with the Kiwi team, a final swim in the pool the next morning and we started our long 25 hour journey back home through Mumbai and Dubai to arrive at Gatwick in time to drive to work on Monday morning. I don't really remember much more after that. Another typical OK Dinghy Worlds was done.

Three in Men Three Boats – David Treglown

UNDERTAKING A SEA PASSAGE IN a small boat requires quite a lot of thought and, I suppose, nerve. There are many things which one has to bear in mind, such as suitable places for an entry in an emergency, equipment for working on the boat while at sea, over night stopping places, routine if gear breaks or skipper becomes disabled by some other means, and also if, by any chance, you are at sea at night, a method of keeping in touch with your fellow boats.

This was worked out by the three of us over a period of about six weeks before the trip, including Sunday trip by car as far as Port Stephens and a thorough examination of the coast from there to Terrigal. After this we considered entry safe at the following points: Fingal Bay, Boat Harbour, northern end of Stockton Bight in a nor'easter, Lake

Macquarie, southern end of Catherine Hill Bay, a small beach north of Norah Head and, of course, Terrigal. We considered places to be avoided were Lake Macquarie on an ebb tide and Newcastle Harbour, as there were very few facilities available at the latter.

Our previous experience in open water sailing amounted to the following: Tony Hill, one season ocean racing, one trip Mosman to Bayview in a Gwen 12, and origin at or of the idea for this voyage. David Treglown, occasional cruises in yachts, Sydney to Pittwater, one trip Mosman to Bayview and one trip Mosman to Yarra Bay in Gwen 12s. John Salmons, no open sea experience in small boats.

Equipment taken on each boat was: 1 lifejacket to be worn at all times; 1 life line to be attached at all times; 1 bucket, plastic, arranged to be used as bailer or sea anchor if needs be; 1 paddle carried on foredeck, could be used as emergency rudder; 1 gallon fresh water; enough food to last three days; handle on bow for towing purposes; sleeping bag and clothing; 1 waterproof torch; 1 compass; spare lacing and miscellaneous tools.

It was also agreed before we left, that each member had power of veto over the other two at any time, and that we would not leave unless a favourable weight of breeze was blowing and each boat was in A1 shape, inspected if necessary, by another member of the party.

The boats were prepared during the week and on Saturday, January 25, we rigged at 8.15 am, the three boats were put into the water and together left the bay. There was quite a fresh westerly blowing and we made good time to the Heads, where the breeze started to kick in a little harder. It was quite a strange feeling to square away in the gusts and realise that New Zealand was our 'eastern shore'. I had jokingly said to a friend going overseas, that I would probably arrive in Canada before him, and at that moment I thought I would!

From the time we left Sydney Heads we could see Cape Three Points. Tony and I took a direct line, but John seemed to think that staying about 1 to 1.5 miles from the coast was best. As it happened, he was right. By the time we arrived at the entrance to Broken Bay, Tony and I were about 5-6 miles off the coast and becalmed. The only noise was the gentle slap of the water on the sides of the boats, we could not see John as his blue sail merged against the shore. About an hour later a light easterly came in taking us to Cape Three Point s, here John's course joined ours from inshore and again we were becalmed. I think there was some breeze around but the short chop shook it out of the sails. I feel a fully battened sail would have been better. John and Tony handled the light conditions better and managed to creep away from me, the 'dud' of the party!

It was very annoying to be left there alone, so I got stuck into some rum, and soon I was feeling much better. Eventually the breeze came and I worked around the Skillion. Having very little wind I decided to come in close to the breakwater - too close. I caught the first wave but the second turned into a wall of white water behind me. Next thing was a terrific 'cart wheel' capsize. When I righted the boat there were people running everywhere on shore, all sure I was going to drown or something, maybe because I had been under the boat releasing my lifeline.

Well, the first day had been completed successfully and there were the boats sitting in front of the Terrigal Sailing Club, safe and sound. Night was spent on the beach until 3.30 am when rain forced us into the boatshed where we shared sleeping quarters with a family of rats: quite good company.

Sunday 26th was wet with winds gusting solidly from the south, not the day to push on. A Bluebird left the anchorage to head south and made heavy weather of it over a sea of white caps, so we retired to the Florida Hotel at 10 am. All day we entertained sailing friends from Sydney who 'just happened to be passing by and thought you might be here' or were astonished when they discovered that we had arrived by water.

Tony seems to be the only person who has been passed whilst sailing his OK by a chap standing on a surfboard on the same wave, quite an achievement. The night was spent in the Terrigal Sailing Club House by kind permission of the members. It seems a shame they no longer race there, but that seems to be the case with many tourist resort clubs.

Monday 27th: again it was blowing but we decided to try it for a short time. There was quite

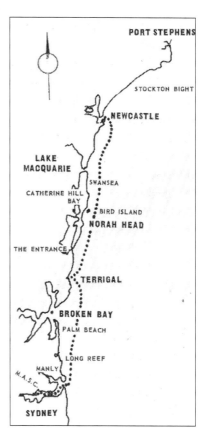

a big sea running but we pushed on, planing over the rollers in sheets of spray, heading north. The Entrance was abeam then Norah Head and some very surprised fishermen, sitting in their boats, wondering where the hell three little sailing boats had come from.

Bird Island was next then we saw Frazer Park. Catherine Hill Bay, where we had thought we might stop overnight went past at 11 am, slightly too early to stop. Off Lake Macquarie the seas were very steep but the boats were behaving well.

My boat was taking water down the mast hole and had discovered that the limber holes were blocked but this was soon rectified with a little help from a screwdriver.

About five miles south of Nobby's, a stainless steel rudder fitting on Tony's boat snapped. It was agreed that I would go on ahead to Newcastle and advise authorities if he did not look like making it but he seemed to be managing alright. John was to stand by in case of further trouble, but they kept going practically as fast as me.

Nearer Newcastle we decided that John would tow Tony into Newcastle rather than bring the boat in under sail, where damage could occur to the boat itself.

I entered the Hunter River and was looking for the closest beach to pull into, when I saw a police launch coming out. I luffed up across its bows and discovered someone ashore had reported a boat in trouble and they were going out to look. John, on seeing the police launch, let go the tow rope and came in under his own power.

He and I both share the opinion that at the entrance to Newcastle were the worst seas we had found. It was the tail of an ebb tide and there were boiling, filthy, muddy seas crashing all around us while the boats were travelling like mad. A rather frightening time and I was very pleased to be on flat water once into the river. We waited for the launch to bring Tony in and accompanied it to the Water Police station where we unrigged.

I cannot say enough about how good they were to us. Most of our gear was wet and we put it out to dry on the boats in their yard. We were allowed full use of their storage space, showers, etc, and were advised of a good hotel to stay at. They were also quite amazed at such small boats coming so far in open water.

John suggested it might be an idea to return to Sydney for my car and trailer when we were offered a trip back in a large motor cruiser leaving early next day, so it was agreed that Newcastle would be as far as we would go.

The trip from Terrigal to Newcastle (about 40 miles) lasted little over five hours, an average speed of 8 knots.

Tony's rudder fitting was replaced the next day and the boats were none the worse for wear after the journey. The only 'troubles' were the blocked limber holes on my boat, my own fault, and Tony's broken rudder fitting which was a fault in the manufacture, as we have heard since of numerous similar fittings breaking. We feel, however, that the OK, although not designed for open water sailing, behaves remarkably well and is suited for the conditions we met.

I have not estimated wind speeds as most people call you a liar if you do. There was, however, a black ball hanging from the Signal Station at Nobby's, which I am told, indicates that the entrance to Newcastle Harbour is not in the most desirable conditions.

The Tiki Story – Adrian Coulthard

THE TIKI IS A PIECE of New Zealand OK history. It came about by the virtue of Craig Pryce winning the last race of the day, at a regatta on Lake Taupo back in 1990s. At the time, Craig would have been one of the younger members in the fleet, and as yet had not mastered the intricacies of sailing the OK fast, so until then he had never won a regatta race before.

To honour the fact that Craig had achieved something (he wasn't in contention for a podium finish), two older members of the fleet, two of the Mannering brothers (Adrian and Nigel) decided to purchase a trophy to be awarded to Craig. As they were in Taupo (a central north island town, at the northern end of Lake Taupo, a tourist Mecca) there were plenty of gift shops selling Kiwiana. Once the brothers spotted the Tiki, they knew it would be perfect. They wanted something gaudy, something obtrusive, and something that would be slightly contentious – the Tiki fulfilled all these requirements.

Originally a wall hung ornament, this Tiki is a glazed ceramic Maori icon, with polished paua shell eyes. The Mannerings added a rope so the Tiki could be worn around the neck like a medal.

That evening, once Craig was wearing the Tiki, the whole fleet celebrated with a drink or two. As the evening progressed, thoughts turned to the Tiki, with various rules being made, starting with once you are wearing the Tiki, you don't take it off until you suit up next morning for yachting. This meant that when the fleet had pre-loaded with drinks, and then moved to the pubs and clubs of Taupo, Craig had to keep wearing the Tiki.

Then the second rule was made up – you can't hide the tiki inside a t-shirt or jumper or put it in a pocket – you have to wear it with pride. Taupo has a rich and historic Maori culture, and with the Tiki being a Maori icon, it would have been quite funny for the elder members of the fleet to watch Craig justifying and explaining why a skinny white fella was wearing a Tiki to the local cuzzies.

Once the regatta was over, the Tiki was returned by Craig to Ade Mannering, who was the original keeper of the Tiki – folklore has it that the Tiki was hung in Ade's eldest daughters bedroom, to ward off evil spirits (or boys).

The kaumatua's (knowledgeable elders) of the fleet decided that the Tiki would be awarded for the regattas on the NZ tour, for winning the final race of the day.

The Tiki is now a well travelled trophy, having been to Thailand, Australia, Europe and Barbados. When going overseas, the Tiki is often placed in the boat of somebody who was too busy to help load the container, as it's thought a little bad luck may be bestowed on that person – maybe a capsize or a BFD.

Over the years, the Tiki has been lost for a number of months, and was found by accident in a random boat shed in Napier. It's also been in the wars a bit, wearing its scars with pride, all representing a different adventure.

There are a number of superstitions related to the Tiki, disrespecting the Tiki has serious consequences – one Tiki winner at a national championships a couple of years ago decided to go home straight after racing, and did not wear the Tiki. Needless to say a Tapu or bad spirit was cast, and the consequences for the sailor meant he was dog tucker on the final day, and went from potentially winning, to not even making the podium. Some sailors won't even touch the Tiki, for fear that they may jinx any chances they

have of winning it in the future. And certainly, nobody has ever worn it that hasn't actually won the right to wear it.

Moving with the times, the Tiki now has its own Facebook page with around 200 friends across the globe. The winner of the Tiki gets posted online along with a photo, and as soon as the results are released, these also get posted. The Tiki has also been known to post various photos and comments to share the fun the NZ OK sailors have, and let the others who are not there know what they are missing.

As a long lasting reminder of winning the Tiki, stickers have been produced, which are awarded along with the Tiki. Luke 'Colt' O'Connell is the current high scorer, with almost 15 wins displayed on his transom.

Over the years there have been a number of worthy winners including, Ade, and Nigel Mannering, Greg Wilcox, Paul 'Gouch' Rhodes, Russ 'Mudsy' Page-Wood, Ben 'Benno' Morrison, Steve 'the lead dwarf' McDowell, Rob Hengst, Jono 'Rabbit' Clough, Chris Fenwick, Dan Slater, Dan 'Bushy' Bush, Matt 'Stechy' Stechmann, Karl Purdie, Alistair Deaves, and a particularly noteworthy winner was Matt 'Munter' Stevens, who managed a yet to be surpassed Tiki and Harpoon double, in Napier, in a side room of the Thirsty Whale pub actually called the Harpoon room.

So if you ever see a Kiwi sailor at a championship wearing a green Tiki around his neck, buy him a drink and have a chat – he may give you some valuable tips about sailing the OK Dinghy fast.

British Nationals, South Shields 1978 – Richard Morell

THE MCINTYRES (PETER, JOHNNY AND Mike) were there. Mike had his Finn in the car park and sailed Clive Farmer's OK 1824, coming fourth with a Delta sail. Rodney did his bar stool trick and fell asleep to wake up and find that everyone and gone home and locked up. Rodney climbed down a drainpipe and then used a boat cover to put on the barbed wire fence so he could break out of the dinghy park.

One evening we got a visit from the coastguard as someone had put a flashing roadworks light on top of Rodney's motor home. It apparently lined up with the entrance to the harbour, and it was only the previous year that they had a coaster up the beach.

By the Wednesday we had drunk all of the beer and the commodore of the club was driving around with a box trailer trying to get more.

During the BBQ evening Alastair McMichael decided to sand the bottom of his boat in the dinghy park near the BBQ. Some of his competitors, who shall remain nameless, decided to use his boat as a table and started putting their greasy fingers on it and stuffing chicken bones down his centreboard case.

Batt Repairs – Rodney Thorne

BLITHFIELD RESERVOIR 1976 – THIS was an excellent weekend for people who liked a lot of wind, probably a Force 6. There was brilliant sunshine and plenty of wind. The black Boyce masts were in their element and working a treat. Dick Batt turned up with a new OK; it had not yet been on the water. If I remember correctly it was 1874, 'Parting Shot'. It had a high deck, and it was amusing to note that when Dick put the centre board in he couldn't get it all of the way down and had to construct an extension to the handle. I think he probably still won the event, sailing for Midland SC.

A Trip Down Memory Lane – Greg Wilcox

A LONG TIME AGO (1981) WHEN we were all younger I was lucky enough to be able to travel to Europe to sail in a few regattas including the OK Dinghy Worlds in Hyères, France. With me was a guy who I had grown up with and had in fact bought my first ever boat from at the age of 13, Earl Berry. We started in London where we picked up our van, of which we were the proud owners of 66 per cent. We had bought the majority share from Murray Jones and Andy Knowles who were 470 sailors and had left the van in storage. It came with two sets of number plates and two starter motors, all of which were needed. The plates were British and Dutch with the idea being you used the Dutch plates in England the British everywhere else. It was something to do with road tax.

Anyway the first job was to put a towbar onto it, which entailed a trip to a wrecker's yard to get some angle iron which we bolted under the back bumper. The New Zealand towball we had brought with us went onto that and we were good to go. We duly collected our boats from Tilbury where they had been sent already packed on the trailer in a 20ft container. I should say we had three boats as another kiwi, Brian Fifield, was to meet us in Hyères.

After an uneventful ferry trip from Harwich to Hamburg we drove up to Kiel for our first regatta. In those days Kiel was one race a day with an 11 o'clock start and really a lot of boats on our course, which was the closest one to the shore. I have no idea about the racing but we had a great time meeting new and old friends. I think the winner was Stefan Järudd who always sailed very well. After Kiel we drove for a few days down to Hyères as the worlds was the next regatta. We were in convoy with the Swedes in case some or all of us broke down. Given the quality of our vehicles in those days it was always a possibility.

In Hyères, Earl and I were staying in a nice B&B along with a crazy Swede called Ingvar Bengtson and a totally crazy Pom turned Aussie, Patrick Whittington. Now Patrick had a sidekick named Chocko (real name Peter Jackson, brother of Mark) and the two of them were never, ever sober. Mind you the rest of us were never far behind. I can't remember if Peter Gale was there too but we all hung out together. At night for our entertainment there was a Tivoli fair with all sorts of weird and wonderful sights like the fat lady: nothing politically correct in those days.

The crazy Danes were also there a lot and in fact the prize they still give out to this day for the guy who gets in the middle spot in their nationals came from there. Peter Brøgger managed to remove an arm with a head attached and he and Frank Hansen spirited it away. We on the other hand concentrated on the ducks. They had a stall where if you could throw a hoop over a duck's head you could take the duck home. Ingvar convinced us we had to save the ducks from certain death by winning as many as we could. The first night we managed to win one duck. The next problem was what to do with it. We thought we could release it somewhere and it could live a long and happy life.

Ingvar put it in the boot of his Volvo and off we drove to find a duck sanctuary. We found a nice backyard with a high fence and the sounds

of happy animals coming from within. We stopped and Ingvar opened the boot. The duck promptly jumped out and ran off down the road leaving an amazing amount of duck droppings over everything in the boot. Sailing gear, sails and what were once clean clothes. By the time we all stopped laughing the duck was gone and it was dark so we decided it was job done and time for a beer.

Next morning on the way to the club there was a traffic jamb. Normally it was no problem. On that day however there was a duck holding up all the traffic by refusing to get off the road. Can't say for sure but we figured it was probably our duck. Anyway the local policeman had a surefire way of moving it by picking it up, wringing it's neck and throwing it in his car. So much for a long happy life but at least it was free for a while. We did however go back and refine our technique and rescue a few more ducks that safely made it over the wall into the peaceful garden where no doubt they also ended up on the table.

The sailing in Hyères was pretty up and down but Peter Gale won from Stefan Järudd and Earl got third. I managed to get my first tie there so it was all good. A good story from there was Per Baagøe was visiting cornersville and the population was one OK and a French fighter jet who thought it would be fun to buzz him. Seeing it was quite light it took some time for Per to empty the water out after he got swamped as the downdraft threw his little boat around. So he went from nearly last to very much last.

After the worlds we went to the French nationals. Of course they were organised for the week after. It was France. It was a lovely little island called Isle des Embiez, and was owned I think by Paul Ricard who supplied vast quantities of Ricard anissette. It tasted awful but got you drunk fast. All I remember from there is in one race they laid the finish line behind Peter Takle who was leading so he ended up back a bit and quite upset and they cancelled the last race as everyone just wanted to lie on the beach with all the Swedish women.

From there the next destination was St Moritz for some ski yachting. Neither Earl nor I could ski so it was to be an educational journey according Mr Bengtson, ski tour guide to the stars. We had a bit of a convoy going with us and a car full of Swedes and another with Ingvar and Major Pradipak, who was from India and had also sailed the worlds. The Swedes had a very full car with four people and sailing gear, so Earl very kindly offered the only woman in there a spot in our large van. Now to be fair they had sort of hit it off for the last few weeks. Anyway she was in our van the whole way and I had to drive for almost all of it. Lucky we had a good stereo.

We finally got to St Moritz and even though it was the middle of summer we had half a metre of snow the first night. It was great if you had some warm clothes. I seem to remember we did some sailing and some skiing and the Swedes won it easily but no idea who it was. Didn't matter, as was great fun.

Next stop was the Dutch nationals. It was a very long drive to get to Hoorn so Ingvar was sharing the driving with Pradipak. It went a bit like this. After four hours Ingvar would say he was tired. They would swap over and after half an hour Pradipak would say he was falling asleep. Ingvar would get out and run around a bit to wake up then resume driving. Pradipak would sit next to him eyes wide open and chatting away. Four hours later the same procedure again, and so it went on. When they arrived Ingvar was totally wrecked and Pradipak who snoozed as well as chatted was fine.

We on the other hand had a slight problem at the border. Of course being lazy we had never changed the plates on the van from the Dutch ones that were on in England and forgotten all about them. We got to the border and got stopped as they wondered why two Kiwis with three boats on a New Zealand trailer were driving a wreck of a Dutch registered van with no current tax paid. We managed to talk our way out of most of it by saying we were passing through on the way to Denmark but it took around six hours after threats of arrest. When the next shift came on the main guy was a sailor. He basically told us to clear off but to change the tyre that was pretty bald. We had a spare but it was being used as a rubbish bin as it had developed a rather large flap in it when it had exploded some weeks before. There was another one which was almost all right but we told the guy we had to find a garage to do it, the reason being was that our car jack would no doubt go up but through the rust and not lift the van. So off we went. Did we change the wheel? No. Did we change the plates? Also no, as we were going to end up back in England at some stage.

After a wet and thunder stormy Dutch nationals (won by Ingvar I think) we went to Sønderborg for the Danish championships, our last regatta. It was a great event as all Danish nationals are. I managed to win with Paul Kirketerp second and Finn Jenson third. I still have no idea how I beat the guy who had won three worlds so there must have been quite some infighting amongst the Danes who obviously let me go.

We had to take our boats back to Tilbury to send them back to New Zealand and Ingvar had the idea to send his boat with ours as the worlds were in Australia the following year. So we just added his to the heap and off we went. It seemed so easy then. We just loaded four boats in the box and sent it off. When they got to New Zealand we just told customs the spare was Swedish and it was going to Melbourne for the next worlds. It never seemed to be a problem. It went to Melbourne and even came back to New Zealand afterwards as a Kiwi boat replacing the one that went under the wharf in the big storm of '82, but that's another story. It was the first Delfs imported to New Zealand and is stilled sailed today.

If you think the van was loaded up in the photo I should say we sold our share back to the 470 guys who put three 470s on it and all their sails and stuff and seven people and drove to Quiberon where David Barnes and Hamish Willcox won the first of their three worlds.

Anyway I cannot vouch for the accuracy of all of this as it is from my fast fading memory. However I can say we all had a lot of fun and laughs travelling in a big group. I am extremely happy to say I am still friends with all these people and we are lucky enough to get together every so often and tell tall tales of the legendary past before we forget.

Rodney's Tales – Richard Morrell and Rodney Thorne

One of the more colourful characters in the class is Rodney Thorne, from the UK. Here are some memories from Richard Morrell and Rodney on his many, many years in the OK Dinghy.

ELIE AND EARLSFERRY 1976 – Rodney sailed OK 1691 and travelled with Bill Bradburn, from South Staffs. Rodney had taken everything with him, even a Black & Decker workmate. Fortunately Bill had a large estate car at the time. A few of the boats got smashed on the rocks after the helms had been rescued during a strong wind against tide situation and heavy seas. One of the boats was only a week old.

Burton sailing Club 1977/78 – On a bright sunny afternoon people were getting a little bored of the light breeze. The boats were gentle bobbing up and down as they were tied up on the landing pontoons. Then someone had a bright idea of getting a house brick, tying a rope through it and attaching it to Rodney's pintle. There was a lot of amusement when Rodney came ashore complaining about there being something wrong with his boat and how it wasn't sailing properly.

South Staffs SC – The wind had died and I no longer needed my weight jacket. So I signalled to a fellow club sailor who wasn't sailing to take it off me. I threw it to him and to his surprise it almost took him off the jetty.

Overy Staithe – We would tear down country lanes in the motor-home towing many OK Dinghies whilst listening to the Boomtown rats, or the Steve Miller Band on Rodney's portable music machine. In those days, before mobile phones and with pub's closing at sensible times it was useful to have a chap like Rodney Tidd having the beers ready on the bar for the time we said that we would arrive. Rod's parent's caravan was next to the pub, which was very handy. They had us dyke running, drinking lots of beer, Whiskey marmalade and Inga-Lisa the drop dead gorgeous Swedish blonde whose boyfriend was a large biker, with a big bike. Her parents (OK sailors) invited us back to their rather grand farm house for a BBQ in a wood at the bottom of their garden. Are contribution was a crate of beer.

Derwent Reservoir 1978 – Windy conditions at Derwent Reservoir in 1978 when the wind speed got up to Force 7 by the end of the one of the races. Most people had already retired and boats needed two or three people to just keep them on their trolleys as they were pulled out of the water. Derwent Reservoir is where the legendary Julian Kettle of South Windermere used to go up wind with his sail up in these conditions, drop it for the downwind leg and then hoist it again. It was very difficult to breathe or see where you were going with so much spray.

Grafham Water Inland Championships 1980 – The event was blown off due to un-sailable wind conditions of Force 7, so we all retired to the Wheatsheaf pub at the end of the drive. I'm guessing this was 1980. We had a few beers and I think it was Martin Goodman who suggested that it would be a good idea to have some food before we had any more beer. Martin was the sensible one. The 'little fellow', Jeremy Wicks, made some noises about being hungry too. So we got menus and by the time we came to order a certain Rodney Thorne was fast asleep on his bar stool. So rather than disturb him we ordered our food. We ate our food. We had a few more beers. Then Rodney sprung back to life and said something along the lines of 'What are we all having to eat then?' to get the surprising reply that we had already eaten a while ago and they might have even stopped serving food.

Felixstowe Ferry – Rodney had arranged with us to stop with Tim O'Leary but Tim had been to a wedding and got side tracked. Rodney decided to sleep in his car and the rest of us had to sleep on the pebbled beach. We got our own back on him the next morning by shaking his car until he got up. One clever clogs half rigged his boat whilst it was still on the road trailer attached to the back of his car. Being a clever so and so he thought he saw a better spot further into the dinghy park, with the big hitters. He jumped into his car and head off with his mast up. Despite people shouting and waving their arms at him he still managed to catch his mast on the overhead cable and pull his boat off the trailer. There's always one, that's his go faster finish gone. There was also a rumour that Rodney managed to drive all of the way from Burton-on-Trent to Felixstowe with his Peugeot 205 Diesel in fifth gear and only fifth gear because the engine had so much torque, or was that just Rodney?

Everything Except The Passport – Peter Scheuerl

WHEN PACKING UP THE BOATS at the end of the 2002 World Championship in Napier, New Zealand, Christian Hartmann had his passport safely stored in his jacket. However he was too clever and figured that he didn't need that jacket until spring in Europe, so he didn't need it in his luggage for flying. So he packed it into his boat and put the boat into the container in Napier. Luckily when we got to Auckland the next day, he double checked if he had everything for travelling, like tickets etc. Of course, everything except the passport was there. Fortunately we still had the whole morning to figure out that there is no German embassy in Auckland, but a consulate, and they were open (luckily not a weekend flight) and they were able to issue an emergency passport.

If I remember right, I think even the 'passport is in a container' wasn't too unbelievable for them, like it happened before. So Christian was only worried a bit, because we wanted to stay in Singapore for a few days, but the emergency passport clearly stated 'not valid to visit any country, only to get straight back to Germany.' But the ever so professional Singaporean customs officers didn't even blink and let him into the country and out again.

Drinking Stories

THE 1994 WORLD CHAMPIONSHIP WAS held in Napier, New Zealand. During the week there was a cocktail evening organised with a professional cocktail maker. All the Australians bought their three bottles of spirits at the airport on the way in and donated them to the event. Some cocktails were more in demand than others, but everyone had a skin full. A certain northern British sailor ended up unconscious in the girl's toilet with no clothes on, with just a shoe covering his modesty.

Performance of the Year 3

ONCE AGAIN IT IS TIME for a class retrospective. Unfortunately many of the stories doing the rounds of various OK dinghy parks and watering holes cannot be published. Far be it for the OK class to prejudice trials, endanger marriages or be responsible for the termination of some potentially lucrative careers.

Before too many people start sweating back to those performances that can be freely spoken about, some of you may remember last year Rod Thorne screwed his boat to his trolley. He did this by the screwing up into the hull method. This year he worked from the other way round, starting from the inside he screwed outwards into the trolley. Recent reports suggest that neither method is actually that effective. Word is that Rod, as I type this, is dotting the 't's and crossing the 'i's of an article on trailers – he has dispensed with the 3" screw method.

We next move to Sweden. At 5 am about half way into the ferry journey home from the worlds in Sweden, Fletcher befriends a moose. It was a 6'6" moose, made of card and called Bjorn. Bjorn was introduced to the rest of the cabin and before daylight many other cabins also knew about Bjorn. Once finished with, the latest victim of the Fletcher's silver tongue was shown the door to the elevator. Poor Bjorn was destined to spend the rest of the journey travelling between floors 1-8.

Burton Beer – Tim Edwards K 1982

I REMEMBER GOING TO A BURTON Sailing Club open meeting, in the mid 1990s, at a guess. We were all sleeping the night in the clubhouse and discovered that we could continue to drink beer after the bar staff had left. With my skinny, boyish (in those days) wrists I could reach through the bar grills that had been locked down, pour a pint into a glass and then decant it into another glass on the outside of the bar. Can't remember my results on the Sunday for some reason.

Torquay in 1983 – Rodney Thorne and Richard Morrell

R ODNEY DECIDED THAT WE NEEDED to make an early start so I arrived at his house the night before. I went to sleep and Rodney was still doing jobs on the trailer. I was to be towing the double trailer behind my new Ford Escort 1.6 Ghia hatchback. The next morning we set off from Burton-on-Trent and I couldn't do more than 40 mph without the rig snaking. I said to Rodney, 'What have you done to this trailer? It's a pig to tow, I can't do more than 40mph, and it's going to take us days to get to Torquay'. After about ten miles I pulled into a lay-by and spotted a very large kerb stone. Rodney thought that I was joking and wasn't too keen, but eventually joined in helping me to lift the kerb stone. We strapped it to the front of the trailer to increase the nose weight. Suddenly I could tow safely at lot faster, and we made good time to Torquay. Rodney arrived with a new boat that he was still fitting out as the event started. He kept leaving his ghetto blaster at the local chandlery for fittings as he didn't have any money on him.

Rodney: "Fart spray isn't a good idea as it almost made our accommodation unbearable. The Royal Torbay Yacht Club had to drop its jacket and tie rule for the week as the Aussies and Kiwis' certainly didn't have any. During the worlds, the week after the nationals, a lot of us got struck down with food poisoning from the seafood at the club. Some people were taken to hospital."

Rodney had us stopping for the week of the worlds in a Leisure 17 yacht in the harbour, not much longer than a 505 dinghy. We had to collect this 'yacht' from up the river Dart, then sail it past Dartmouth and round to Torquay. As we came to Brixham, Rodney insisted on frightening the locals by going ashore for an ice cream. I think he really wanted to have a look at the replica of the Golden Hind. I can't forget the

Aussie's getting down to some AC/DC in the Royal Torbay Yacht Club. "Shook me all night long".

On the way back the new tyres that Rodney had fitted to his road trailer failed, one after another, whilst we were on the motorway. Fortunately my launching trolley wheels were road trailer wheels and got us home.

Drinking Jackets

ULF BRANDT WAS FAMOUS FOR wearing his drinking jacket at after race drinking evenings. It was a lightweight sailcloth jacket made by Green that protected him from the beer fights as the evenings wore on. He always stayed dry while everyone around him got wet.

The UK team decided it was time to plan their revenge after an eventful opening ceremony at the 1994 Europeans in Neustadt. No one can remember who started it, but the Danish team got involved in a food fight with the British team in a large marquee. It was all going a bit too far and then one of the Danes appeared at the back of the tent with a fire hose. Needless to say both teams were on strict orders from the organisers to behave for the rest of the week or risk disqualification.

The UK team got their revenge a year later at the worlds in Felixstowe Ferry Sailing Club when in a choreographed operation, they simultaneously donned identical Ullman drinking jackets and drowned Ulf with whatever they had left in their glasses.

Just like Kiel – Peter Scheuerl

IN 1993 THE WORLD CHAMPIONSHIP was racing in Puck, Poland. I can't quite remember which race, but it was probably Race 6 and we had really funny and very shifty conditions, and light winds. Bo-Staffan

Andersson was somewhere in the middle of the fleet at the last leeward mark. A short time later, everybody was drifting along upwind, not hiking, and one boat comes out of the far right corner, planning on a tight reach around the whole fleet to finish in the top. Bo-Staffan's comment after the race on how he saw that "I sailed in Kiel before…" He went on to win his fourth world title that week. At that time in Kiel the OKs were still on Area Delta, right in front of the marina, where huge shifts were normal, especially in westerly winds.

The Full Monty – Adelaide 1998

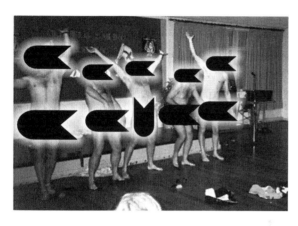

THE BRITS "…PRACTICED ALL WEEK for it. The movie had just come out."

"About a minute after this photo was taken Hamish Fenwick went after them with a fire extinguisher."

"Was too drunk to remember much as it was the night we drank around 300 vodka stolis and Fletcher was found in a ditch with Hitz."

The Prizegiving to End all Prizegivings – Peter Jackson

THE 1982 WORLD CHAMPIONSHIP PRIZEGIVING at Black Rock has gone down in OK folklore as epic, and the fact that the legend, reputation, infamy survives to this day is testament to the proceedings that evening.

Some background…

It had been a difficult week (see photo). The normal Port Phillip seas breezes hadn't really come, and the week was more dominated by a counteracted northerly flow. The days racing proceeding the night in question had been called off with 40 knot northerly winds, ending the

series with five heats in total. The northerly airflows made it hot – very hot. It made everyone very .... THIRSTY.

But the action was only building, as we hung around for the eventual abandonment in the mid afternoon, and then keener types started packing up in the heat. Some started on pre-refreshment.

Remember we were all hot and getting THIRSTIER.

Disclaimer from now on – memories may start to get inaccurate from now, due to heat, consumption and the 35 years since it happened. If you get mentioned and you weren't there, sorry. If you were there and get mentioned, and don't want others to know what you were doing, sorry. If I get some things wrong – I've done my best.

The evening started like most other prizegivings – people you never normally see in neat clothing-long trousers-deodorant-combed hair were all there, engaging in pleasant conversation; partners were there, club officials, even some sailing association types.

But, due to thirstiness, there was a pace being set, in particular a table by the front windows near the balcony with some young Aussie and Wellington-Napier kiwi guys (from memory) but there might have been certain younger Danish and German guys involved as well.

After the official prizegiving – that I believe was notable for a full distribution of trophies even though only five heats were sailed (I thought that was nice) and some of the more senior people from the club and the official guests had departed (I hope they had), then the spirit of competition remained very much in the room. There certainly were beers; there might have been rum buckets. I can't remember what form the competition took, but it must have been competitive. There was some sort of singalong at some point I think. Ingvar Bengtson was playing the blues on the battered old piano in the club and really got the party going.

But it just seemed to get crazier and crazier and later and later – and no-one seemed to want to leave.

I seem to remember the main protagonists for the evening were the, then, Wellington guys, Greg Wilcox, Joe Porebski, Earl Berry, Ade Mannering, Greg Stephenson, Andre Blasse, from Australia, Reemt Reemtsma (he didn't have a choice as he was staying at my place), Stig Westergaard, Ingvar Bengtson Stefan Järrud, the Nilssons and Mats Caap from Sweden. Apologies if I've forgotten anyone.

From what I remember we had really a lot of drinking races with pots of beer. Joe Porebski was the man in charge and he called the rules and made them up as he went along. The kiwis won mainly due to the ability of the Mannering brothers who made it seem like they had two less people in the team. There were a lot of 'general recalls' and the combined European team did a great job of staying on their feet afterwards. Obviously we had to get the mops out to clean the floor and the walls. The pool table was in constant use with jugs of beer on the outcome of each game.

At some stage, the Black Rock club guys just volunteered to stay and keep the bar open long after all the event staff had left. I'm not sure how many of them there were but it was much appreciated at the time – a marathon effort. I think they might have been thirsty as well

And so it continued – some guys went quiet for a while and then came back – others had a little kip in the corner, but came back – others drifted off really late but then seemed to come back, showing up to prizegiving at 3 am and finding it still going – we were thirsty.

This may have been the last outing of the Kiwi Valiant – for those too young to remember the Valiant was a vehicle of dubious quality made in Australia in the 1960s and early 70s. They were famous for having a dash mounted push button automatic.

The Wellington Kiwis had bought the Valiant to get them around while in Melbourne. They probably didn't pay much for it – good thing too.

Anyway, at some stage after the prizegiving – might have been 4 am but may have been later – the just recently crowned world champion, Rick Dodson and about seven or eight others thought a spot of car park circle work was in order. The Valiant was duly enlisted for the task – and that was it for the Val – bang-crash-wheel missing-radiator pushed backed 18 inches – but nothing else in the car park damaged. Luckily the walls of the road down to the car park are lined with strong and sturdy boulders as the mighty Valiant was bounced from side to side up and down the drive a few times. They were simpler days then. It stayed down in the Black Rock car park with the doors open (not able to be closed) windows broken, and full of empty beer cans, for about a month after the series before the council removed it.

Then, just before sunrise, there was the idea floated that we should get up on the roof and watch out to the east for the sun. Might have been Greg Stephenson's idea, maybe Joe Porebski, Greg Wright, aka bubble or maybe Andre.

As you may be aware, the BRYC clubrooms are a two storey building, with a gabled roof, the architects of which had thoughtfully designed with a 130-degree angle at the apex, just the right angle (apparently) to place chairs along the top to watch the sun. So the chairs came out of the clubrooms and ended up on the roof, along with some keen sunrise admirers.

I'm not sure how we actually got up there, but the view was great and no-one (amazingly) fell off.

Then, at about 7.30 in the morning, there was a need to breakfast – so in peak hour traffic, in my Toyota Crown wagon and I think one of the yellow Swedish Volvo loan cars (they were sponsored), we turned up at the Hampton St 7-11 (no longer there) where pies, sausage rolls and donuts were order of the day. I remember Joe commenting that the pies could have been hotter, but this was when 7-11s actually opened between 7 and 11 – they hadn't been on long enough.

The last thing I remember when leaving the club with some takeaway beers was looking up and seeing two chairs on the roof with some empty beer cans beside them, a visual testament to the 1982 prizegiving.

Fly Tipping

ONE MORNING, NOT SO LONG ago, at about 3.00 am, a group of Kiwi OK Dinghy sailors in various states of inebriation desired to get rid of an OK that had reached the end of its useful life and was now just taking up valuable shed space. Rather than the sensible solution of taking it to the dump they decided that it needed one more adventure and drove it 50 km into the Napier hills to the Mohaka Bridge. The drop to the river is about 200 feet and with great effort, and a surprising amount of luck at not getting caught, they lifted the boat off the trailer and dropped it over the side.

Two weeks later, a sailor who was new to the fleet came across an OK on his father in law's farm, some 20 km downstream from the Mohaka Bridge.

Amazingly the boat was undamaged. He then hatched a plan to restore the boat and return it to the club. Unfortunately the plan got forgotten and the boat, probably like many others, lies at the back of a barn in the middle of nowhere.

Aft is Fast – Sten Waldö

IN THE EARLY DAYS OF the class many people were struggling to meet the 72 kg minimum weight for the OK, while still making the bottom stiff and strong enough.

I had read somewhere about efforts in the UK to build composite hulls while avoiding normal wood. This did not work well with plywood because it sucked up humidity and expanded leaving the bottom of the hull wavy. So I did my own and we built a number of boats that spring including my S 1510 for the Hayling Island world championship. On the side I also worked 'hard' on my MSc.EE studies, which obviously left no time for sailing.

I arrived at Hayling Island in 1965 with the boat just fresh from decking and painting by Henriksen and found out the complete weight was only 60 kg, but was lucky enough to find 12 kg of lead, which I fixed all way back in the boat.

Why there? Paul Elvstrøm had once told me, that in the early days they experimented with the Finn weight distribution and found out, that with the weight all the way aft, those boats were by far the fastest planing.

At the same time, however, it called for some physical power to hike out towards the bow upwind. Well, back then with no rules for maximum or location of corrector weights; I put it all aft, just in front of the rudder.

Regarding the shape of our composites, we utilized the tolerances fully to make the bottom keel line as straight as possible from the centerboard to the stern and the front bow area as full as possible. The intention was to create a design for the maximum planing speed.

I put some mast in the boat and grabbed a sail from the year before.

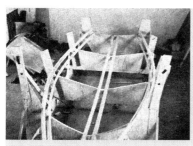

The building of Sten Waldö's
S 1510 using a jig • Over: Sten Waldö
chases Göran Andersson, the eventual
winner in Hayling Island

We started the championship racing inside Chichester Harbour – there was too much wind out on the intended course area – and I got a miserable 15th place.

Next day we were out with the waves and a good breeze, about 15-20 knots. I did three second places and was leading the field after four races. Then the wind went away and, also with that, my luck. I withdraw from one race (hitting a mark) and had a 69th, all for a total of tenth overall.

Now, what's interesting is the following.

In the second race about four or five guys, including me, were late out and we were towed to the start line by a motorboat. We started three minutes after the gun. I still crossed the finish line in second. Actually, in the Swedish OK magazine '*OK bladet*' it was reported how I was moving up, run after run from three minutes behind to second place just 20 seconds behind the race winner.

That boat was so fast downwind planing, that I basically only needed to hang on to it, keeping it balanced, of course, but I could sail in any weather with my eyes closed back then. It was kind of natural for me, but it was just ridiculous, how I just rushed past everybody on the run like a rocket, while upwind I was able to do fine because of the wind and with similar speed to the other top guys.

That S 1510 was by far the fastest OK around that season. Only the sailor in it was not up to the mark to helm it the way it deserved.

Both S 1510 and S 1668 built by me on this jig in 1965 are still around and sailing in Sweden

By the way, I did finish my studies and got my MSc.EE in 8.5 years as opposed to the normal 5.5 years, but I had some fun.

We'll Meet Again – Ralph Eriksen

I JOINED THE OK FLEET AT the Worlds in 2012 where it was held in Vallensbæk, Denmark.

Even in Vallensbæk, where there hardly was any wind, I managed to capsize in almost every single race and dropped out of the race because of the time limit. But it was also during these capsizes I got the feeling that this class is very special – sailors who watched me in the water, struggling to get up sailed by and gave me a lot of encouragement by shouting;

"Come on Ralph – you can do it."

"Get up on the horse again…don't give up."

…and much more that encouraged me to keep on going. This kind of moral support from former, current and coming champions plus the rest of the fleet did it for me…I got infected by the wonderful OK disease and, fortunately, I haven't found any cure for this great disease.

I also realised that the OK fleet is a fleet with lots of spaciousness. Sailors like me are given the same respect as the top 10 sailors; we are allowed to participate in events like the Worlds, the Europeans and, and, and like any other – and remember we are on the water, struggling much more of the time than the top 10 guys who often already had their shower and had changed their clothes when I got in…and the shower was often only in cold water, the top 50 had used all the hot water. But I was always smiling inside, because I was allowed to do the best I can do with clothes on…sailing the OK Dinghy.

I also hate to mention any names here, because for every name I mention, there will be at least 15 names that won't be mentioned, and I consider the whole fleet to be good guys and I see you all as friends. Where I write about specific episodes I'll either mention the name or write something that everyone can understand.

On the course, at the start or by the marks, I have always tried to stay away from the fast guys. I would hate to be the one who ruined someone's chance of winning by doing something wrong or disturbing someone's race, but a (very) few times something went wrong…suddenly I was up there; at the first mark. I felt the adrenalin pumping in my old veins, I started sweating, getting an eye on every finger; and luckily it only took 15 minutes to be where I belonged…when I was slowly, but steadily falling behind, Lauge yelled at me, "Come on Ralph get into battle", but I was deaf, I did not want to be in the middle of a bunch of top 10 sailors, and luckily enough, a few minutes later I made the most photogenic capsize, got mud inside my mast, on my sail and in my head.

Yes this happened at the Europeans on Steinhuder Meer – a great championship, where Ossie had been working like an ant to make one of the best, maybe THE best event ever: food, beer, party, a wonderful trip to a small island, a great party. And still Ossie had time to sail, to talk – I don't think the smile ever left his face during this event. Thanks Ossie, this event has become a beacon for every event to follow. It was also here that I was overtaken by the leaders. I turned around and saw that the winner was the sailing legend Lind. He showed his fist when he passed the finish line and I stood up and applauded him very loud, maybe to loud, because the course dinghy came by and asked me if everything was ok, so I kept on and made it to the finish line just in time.

The OK Class is filled with personalities, who make my daily life a bit brighter when I go down memory lane. I'll mention a few here:

There is this kinky sailor from a Scandinavian Country, always with a perfect tan and maintained curls, no names mentioned but he has something to do with real estate I think, when the sun is there he sails in hi-cut hotpants and a very small shirt which shows his biceps. Always smiling and ready to have a talk.

If the class gave points for elegant hiking, I think number 6 would be a clear winner – next time you see him take a look at his hiking style on the water and his lines when he is ashore. I think he might be a rope'n'knot fetishist…but he is always asking how things are going and ready to help you, but beware of his temper, if it comes out he can lift you and your boat out of the water. I saw it in Vallensbæk.

The opposite of number 6 is a certain English guy, I think he is a sailmaker…he Hunt's you down with smartness and muscles, as if he was making a work-out, and of course always nice, smiling and humble, as humble as you can be when you just won the Worlds.

Germany has one of the greatest 'rockers. He must love to go hiking in the mountains, because his pumping skills are refined in such a way, that it must come from pumping his air mattress when he sleeps in the mountains. And if the Jury shows him the yellow flag, he looks at them with the most innocent face and asks, "What….me?"

My good friend Bo Petersen (whose name has to be mentioned, otherwise you wouldn't know who I'm talking about) is 'The Special One' in the OK class. He is always amongst the favourites, and always making a good result. But don't go near him just before or after a race, he uses a special kind of mindfulness developed by himself, I would call it ready-to-beat-them-war-ness, and if Bo makes a mistake on the course you all know it, his voice can reach stormy heights. Bo is dedicated, he has his target (to win) and he is always focused. But don't misunderstand me, Bo is a good guy, filled with empathy and always ready to help you go faster. Take a discussion about politics and society with Bo; you have to be sharp and know what you are talking about, but he respects you and listens to you. He also has quite some knowledge about music and has quite a good voice; why not ask him to sing a song next time you meet him?

At Lind Classic in Hellerup, I had one of those days again, where something went wrong. I got a new mast and a new sail, and was actually feeling that I've gained some speed. I was fast upwind, made a good downwind, my speed was as good as the best, at the bottom mark, just before the last upwind I was in fifth place. I was on the beat, sweat in my eyes; everything was pumping in my body…round the mark, and no speed, just drifting away, did I have something on my centerboard? On my rudder? Anything wrong with the mast, the sail? Then a silent voice reached me; after getting in front of me…seeing me dropping down to 15th or so place, Mik-Mak whispered, "Ralph, we are going upwind… you have to get your centerboard down!" Well remember to stay calm, even if you are at the front, and never trust your so called friends; they'll beat you if they can.

The class is in a state of constant development, new hull shapes, new sail-cuts and new masts. The mast and the sail is the engine, as I have been told. Stiff, soft, sideways bending and, and, and. We have a sailor in Denmark whose approach to sailing is almost scientific. He is talking a lot about the progressive mast. I've tried to understand what he is talking about, and guys beware, do only ask him about the shape of your sail or your mast bend if you are tired. He will start a lecture that will stop your brain from working and close your eyes. But he knows a lot about car painting, he always has cigarettes (good to know Greg) and his wife makes the best breakfast with eggs and everything, so he is a good man to know.

In Denmark we actually have two boat builders now. One of them, not the one from Vejle, has a long and good reputation, not only in Denmark, but worldwide. His boats are State Of The Art. When it comes to measurements and rules his knowledge is second to none and he is always ready with good advice, some help, some bits and pieces to help you go sailing. His abilities regarding the OK Dinghy are not to be questioned, just like his party abilities. If you need a beer, a good laugh, some good stories, good music…go to his car, just follow the music and the laughter. As my youngest daughter said, when she met him at the Nordics in Præstø;

"I don't know if he loves sex, drugs and rock'n'roll – but he certainly loves sailing, beers and rock'n'roll...his team should be named "the rock'n'roll sailing team".

She is still talking about Præstø and how responsible, grown up, highly qualified sailing athletes in tip top shape were able to knock down a rock festival within a few hours and party all night through, firmly led by the boat builder and then go out sailing the next day – and the funny thing is that he often make the best results after a wet night.

There is also this guy, I think he is English and his job is something with writing, journalism or...?? I still remember meeting him the first time, it was at the Worlds in Vallensbæk; Stefan Myralf introduced me to him and I thought he was from Eastern Europe somewhere. When he speaks his voice is very, very, very, very low and he sort of cuts the words or speaks a dialect that is not easy to understand for the untrained ear. But when you get to know him, it turns out that he is a hard working, really nice guy, a great sailor and one of those who has a big share in the way the class is growing and developing all over the world. I think the class has a lot to thank him for. But could anyone please teach him to articulate a bit more when he is speaking, you know conversation promotes understanding, but only if you can hear what the man is talking about.

There are so many stories and so little space. I have met people from Sweden, Denmark, Germany, Holland, Belgium, France, England, Australia, New Zealand and you have all left some marks in me. Dear friends, girls and guys for me it has been a privilege to get to know you all, a privilege to have been racing with and against you all, a privilege to have introduced my wife and youngest daughter to you all. I wish the class the best, I wish you all the best. Have fun out there where men become boys and women mermaids.

Polish Invitation – Peter Scheuerl

IN 1986 REEMT REEMTSMA, SECRETARY of the German association at the time, contacted several east European sailing associations and asked if there were any OK Dinghy regattas we would be able to attend as West Germans. Responses were a bit mixed, Russia was not euphoric but sort of OK with the idea, but offered regattas too far away, apparently East Germany didn't even answer... But the Polish sailing association was very keen, and that was probably the reason so many Polish sailors stayed in the class after the Eastern Bloc fell apart, as they knew that there were strong fleets in the west as well.

The Polish national association wrote invites for us and exemptions from the mandatory money exchange, so we got our visa quickly and had a stamp in our passports so say that we were important people...

So in the Autumn of 1986 several OK sailors left Hamburg and Kiel in three cars with several OKs on trailers to go to a lake close to Warsaw.

Unfortunately the roads gave us some grief, while the East German motorways got really bad as soon as we had left the Hamburg-Berlin transit part of it, and we had to slow down as there were steps in the motorway between the concrete parts it was made from. While the steps went always down, it was a constant hammering of the material.

Once across the Polish border, the roads were nice and smooth, but went up and down over small hillocks, so that at the bottom the cars and trailers where pushed into the suspensions. Sure enough the rattling and then the hillocks were too much for one of the trailers. Travelling at night, it was quite a spectacle of sparks when the axle broke and the metal was pulled over the asphalt.

So in the middle of the night on a country road in Poland, we had to unload the boats onto the grass beside the road, unload one of the boats from a car's roof and put the trailer on the car instead.

Reemt was quick enough in thinking and grabbed all cigarettes and alcohol we had in the cars and set off with one of the others. In the next village, at 3 am, they found someone on a motorbike. That person saw the problem and knew the solution; there was a railway workshop not far. So they went there and with welding equipment slightly over-sized – one comment was that it was hard to not melt half the trailer's axle with it – they fixed the axle in perfect style in return for a carton of cigarettes and a bottle of alcohol.

At the sailing event we all stayed in army barracks close to the lake – it would have been impossible to think of East Europeans staying in western barracks without any security fuzz at this time – we had a pretty good event, made many new friends in Poland and learned a lot about the local way of drinking tea (which mainly meant waiting for the tea to cool down while drinking a lot of Vodka).

On the way back, not far from the same spot, a truck ran into the back of the same trailer. The trailer made it and was still used later, but one of the boats – Norbert Petrausch's – was incorporated into some steel frames of the trailer, so he had to get a new boat – the purple 'Pitty-Platsch' he still owns today.

The Mother of all Storms – Greg Wilcox

IT WAS 1982 – THE year of the storm and the only time I thought I was in real trouble on the water.

It was a nice sunny day in Melbourne and the fleet was out on Port Phillip Bay for the invitation race of the Australian Nationals held at Black Rock Yacht Club the week before the World Championships. There were probably around 60 OKs sailing. Not everyone was there yet as it was the warm up event. We were maybe 3 km downwind from the club and lining up for the start. In the distance there was a rather big black line of clouds coming our way and in those days there was no forecasting in real time so no one was really aware of how strong the oncoming front would be.

The first start was a general recall but half the fleet was already heading for the shore as it was getting quite fresh by then. The wind was up around 20-25 knots. Some of us stayed around waiting for the next start when it was abandoned and then it got even windier, up to around 35-40 knots. At this stage we were pretty much in survival mode apart from Leith Armit had reached the club by now but decided to go upwind a bit further and then he came back downwind practicing some gybes.

I was heading upwind and it was not so bad; hard work but sailable, just, when suddenly it got really windy. I was blown straight over. When I got the boat upright I was just hiking to keep it upright and the tiller was across the other side. There was no way could I get in to reach it without capsizing again. I didn't want to do that as my old boat had no bulkhead in the front and was pretty much open as there were holes in the cockpit bulkhead to let the water out. In this case it was going in.

As I hiked there pondering my fate I looked to leeward and there was 16 year old Anthony Reynolds standing on the foredeck of his boat lifting the mast out. He didn't want anything bad to happen to the boat as Peter Gale the defending World Champion was supposed to sail it in the worlds the next week. I thought that if Arnold (his nickname) could do that then I could get in to the shore.

Luckily (or stupidly) I sailed in bare feet in those days so I hooked the centerboard line with my foot and pulled the board around half up. Then I got the mainsheet and just pulled it in causing the boat to tack. I just grabbed the tiller on the way and was off again. After some time sailing upwind with the board around three-quarters up and almost no tension on the mainsheet the water was gone and the wind had died to a steady 40-45 knots.

Now, at Black Rock it can be a bit tricky getting in as there is an old wreck in the water outside the club, the Cerberus, and you can either sail between it and the reef or around it. To get in on that day it was a reach through the gap then directly downwind to the ramp. After making it to the wreck I feathered it through the gap then just let everything go and drifted into the beach where a lot of guys were waiting in the surf to help.

When I pulled the sail down I found the leech was coming apart and the sail was ripping across next to a seam. Another five minutes of flapping and it would have just ripped in half and I would have been going nowhere. I have to say the beer tasted pretty good after that.

The rescue guys did a great job that day. They took 18 sailors off their boats and just left the boats to drift. People first, boats second. The next day they went and found the boats. All but one were fine. The one that wasn't was Lachie MacLean's (a Kiwi) and it went under the wharf at Mordiallic. The boys found it in the morning. There was a bit of mainsheet floating up and when they pulled it in they got the boom, what was left of the sail, the mast, the control lines and the cleats with little bits of deck around them. Basically they picked up the bits and put it in the boot of the car. Completely destroyed.

[When Lachie MacLean got separated from his boat he thought he would drown as there was no one anyone near him. The storm passed and he was seen by an Opti sailor who sailed over and rescued him and probably saved his life. He later found out that there was a fisherman called Lachie MacLean that drowned on Port Phillip Bay, 100 years previously.]

John Derbyshire was sailing Earl Berry's boat and he just went straight to the nearest beach and got a local guy to help him put the boat under a tree and tie it down. We all thought he was dead and gone but it just took him a while to walk back to the club. The next morning he just walked back to the boat and sailed it round to the club.

For those who think it may not have been that bad the top recorded gust was 67 knots.

Around two weeks later we were all ashore on the last day of the worlds wondering why we were not sailing as it looked like a lovely breeze. The PRO just said he had heard another front was coming, so advised us to tie the boats down. Normally we might have scoffed at this however we did it. Half an hour later it was over 50 knots and raining. The beers started and the pool games continued and the party went on until 8 am the next morning. But that's another story for someone else to tell.

Another Storm – Sten Waldö

The 1964 International Swedish OK Championships was held at Skälderviken in southern Sweden. The International Champion was Henning Schachtschabel, but the National Champion was Sten Waldö.

I HAD JUST STARTED RACING OKS two years before and 1964 was my first time sailing in Sweden. I went there with my second self-built boat competing against the mighty Marinex team, the champions from the year before. Well, things were about to change.

There was a race of crucial importance to me.

In one of the races, on a rather long reach, during the final flat run down we were hit by a serious hail storm from behind. Back then we had no compass, so with zero visibility I just hung on and did my best to keep the boat going in what I believed would be the right direction to the bottom mark. After maybe 5-6 minutes things cleared up and – I was all alone.

The other guys were all gone, off to the sides, capsized or doing their best to save the situation in other ways. I found the bottom mark just in front of me, rounded and had a nice but lonely tack up to the finishing line.

We had 144 boats on the starting line that year. I sailed D 510 and the following year had S 1510, which I got around 2-300 numbers too early. The OK class was huge in Sweden back then.

Göran Dahlström was defending champion and was widely expected to win again. He was judged to be a heavy wind specialist – but I beat them all in that. Heavy wind sailing is more technique, physics and mental strength than anything else. I had all of that, while not being a very good sailor by other means. They protested to Svenska Seglarförbundet after the races and wanted to disqualify me for sailing a Danish registered boat. Their protest was turned down, but the rules were later amended to allow Swedish participation in Swedish registered boats only.

That Happy Feeling – Nick Craig

Nick Craig is the most successful OK Dinghy in the history of the class with a record five world titles to his name, so it is fitting that this tribute to the class ends with some of Nick's stories.

I LOVE SAILING THE OK AND not just the boat but the complete package – fantastic international racing, great socials, good fun people to spend time with and lifelong friends. I do have a dirty secret though. I sailed a Laser for six months straight after leaving my youth class, the Cadet. After 26 years of OK sailing and beer, it's possible that I have a few dirty secrets but this is the only one I'm planning on sharing.

After growing up in Cadets, the RYA gave me the brilliant advice to race a horrible-to-sail, boring boat, the Laser. Following a tedious day on the water, Laser socials consisted of a post sail protein shake and press-up competition in the clubhouse. The RYA's splendid advice risked yet another sailor dropping out of the sport in the youth to adult racing transition.

So I thought I'd try something different and turned up to my first OK Dinghy event – the 1991 Inlands at Grafham. My first impression of the fleet was how friendly and down to earth everyone was. The bar was great fun and I learnt some new songs I could share at college assembly. I left my boom behind at the event and discovered that the Deaves provide a handy tidy-up-and-deliver-leftovers-after-sailing service.

In short, it was a fleet with some pretty outrageous, disgusting animals, so I thought I might do a bit more OK sailing. Little did I know back in 1991 the journey this would take me on.

In 1995, I sailed at my first OK Worlds at Felixstowe. I loved the international racing. I got to see very different approaches to the sport by sailors from around the world, a mix of equipment and cultures. The socials were once again a lot of fun. The OK Worlds was the best event I had done with the perfect mix of highly competitive racing and friendly socials, which remains true to this day. A home worlds is a fantastic thing – a three hour drive for some of the best racing there is. I came 21st. I was pleased with the result but I could see that there was a big gap to the front.

I got the bug for International OK sailing and proceeded to sail in 17 Worlds in a row.

By 1999, I had been stuck at about 20th at the worlds for a few years and I had worked out that corporate life was well, not that exciting. So I

Clockwise from top left: With Gautama Dutta and Nitin Mongia; with Mongia and Ben Morrison at the 2003 world's prizegiving; with Dan Bush and Graeme Lambert in 2002 in Napier; failing at limbo dancing in Goa.

took two months unpaid leave and sailed the OK almost every day. This did the trick – I came third and have been knocking around the top 10 ever since then.

At the 1999 Worlds in Neustadt, I had to come back from a disqualification in Race 1 for having my main halyard being half an inch above the black band. After some time (months), I realised this was a useful lesson in boat preparation – not an area of natural strength for me and at big events an area I have focused on since then. Without the Race 1 disqualification, I would have been near to winning it. But actually winning the OK Worlds appeared to be elusive in the following years.

I came second in Poland in 2000 after an interesting match race, fifth in Sweden in 2001, eighth in New Zealand in 2002, third in India in 2003 and second at Parkstone in 2004.

After a decade of trying and countless hours on the water and in the gym, I finally won the OK Worlds in 2005. This was and will always be THE biggest high in my sailing life. :-)

More recently, the 2013 Worlds in Thailand was the perfect event in glorious sailing conditions with lively socials but I didn't completely love the event. I was stale of OK sailing. I found that hard to understand because the OK is a great boat, the people are fun and friendly and I'd had such fantastic times. But even something as good as OK sailing can still be overdone. So after 17 Worlds in a row, I largely quit OK sailing for four years. It was a good call. I came back to the mighty OK enjoying it more, I'd gained good experience in other boats that I could apply to the OK, I was hungrier and sailed an OK better than I had for a decade.

My warm up event for the 2017 Barbados Worlds was the one of the best events on the sailing calendar, Medemblik. I was slow. I knew that would probably be the case with borrowed kit but I went anyway. My event objectives were to win every start, be the quickest downwind and drink some beer. I came away fourth and way off the lead but I hit my personal objectives.

Whilst the result was frustrating, this turned out to be an excellent foundation for Barbados. With my favourite rig back and the quickest OK I've raced from Simon Cox, I had speed again. I had pushed the starts in training and at Medemblik which helped me stay in the front starting row in Barbados.

The 2017 Worlds in Barbados was much closer than it looked – I took nine points on last beats. The persistence and never give up attitude from 10 years of not winning it helped me through. We started Race 4 in 25 knots and I struggled. The one part of my event preparation which hadn't gone well was weight gain – with middle age, proper weight gain is harder. I had only managed to hit 87kg whereas I think 90 is the perfect worlds course weight. In Race 4, despite a lot of effort and pain, I was 11th to the windward mark with Jim and Luke in the top few. This race was potentially an event turner. But I was lucky – a key feature of winning any event – the wind dropped considerably and I came back downwind to finish third in that race.

Luck plays a massive part in winning any championship. Luck has been on my side in every event I have won. However, being in the top five at a championships isn't luck. That is all about preparation. Who comes where in the top five is down to luck, who hits their rhythm that week and mental resilience in the crunch last couple of days

I love OK sailing – both the people and the boat are great. The OK is more than a boat, it's a community. The OK is a class people join and stay in for decades. That is such a good sign, sailors love the OK and I love it. This longevity in the class means the OK has a class infrastructure that is for sure second to none. People sail the OK, and put back in when they have more time later in life. The D-One is also a great boat to sail but the class is struggling because it is young and most of the sailors are family people with jobs so have very little spare time.

The OK is my home boat. When I step in an OK, it feels like I am back to my roots and sailing family. This happy feeling seems to be affecting the whole OK sailing world. In Barbados, after the measurer had pulled me up for a spot check and went over my boat, he apologised for the inconvenience and bought me a beer, which was cold. How things have moved on since my 1999 disqualification.

I also love the OK as a boat. It is both frustrating and rewarding. After 26 years in an OK, you'd think I'd have boat familiarity. In my other 'home' boat, the Enterprise, I know I can jump straight in and be competitive. That can't be done in an OK. OKs have a narrow and nebulous groove upwind and you need to find a rhythm downwind or you just dig a hole. I was slow for five of my seven months in the build-up to Barbados. The mighty OK smacks you when you have it wrong or even just not quite spot on. It is hugely frustrating at times but massively rewarding when she is on song.

I have lot of stories of OK sailing over the years. I have promised to keep this clean so I won't mention Burt's bath, Ken's sofa or the Highcliffe prizegiving.

No other class of boat, or probably any sport, would have taken me to most of Northern Europe, New Zealand, Thailand, India, Australia and Barbados giving me the chance to see cultures up close in a way that no normal holiday would. For example, if you went to Goa on a beach holiday you would probably never realise that India is so corrupt. At the 2003 Worlds, we had a few issues releasing our OKs from the container. I remember well a speedboat ride to a dodgy customs house for a chat with an official. Whilst I was talking, one of the Indians handed over a pile of rupees and suddenly all the paperwork and hassle disappeared.

My favourite ever prizegiving also happened in Goa. It was at a 5-star hotel with unlimited drinks; so what could possibly go wrong? The evening entertainment was provided by amazingly flexible limbo dancers. After a few drinks, the OK fleet joined in with some hilarious results. Suffice to say, we need to stick to OK sailing. A hot evening and a lot of drink inevitably resulted in many people ending up in the posh swimming pool. Security did not like this so the 5'5" bouncer came to have a go at me (not sure why I was deemed the responsible adult) so I pushed him in the pool to cool him off. After the prizegiving, we discovered the hotel bar, which turned out to be where Indian film stars and supermodels hang out. I have no idea why none of them wanted to dance with wasted, dripping wet OK sailors.

Whilst I am OK-less right now (first time in 26 years), I will always sail an OK. The fleet is packed with inspirational role models – Alan Atkin is still enjoying sailing the OK fast at my home club into his late 70s. Hopefully I have at least 30 more years sailing this fine boat and drinking beer with friends.

▶ ▶ ▶

ACKNOWLEDGEMENTS

WITHOUT THE CONTRIBUTIONS AND IDEAS of many people across the world this book would not have been possible. It was a collaborative effort from former and current sailors to create a fascinating picture of the class and its sailors. So huge thanks to the following: Dan Ager, Claes Ahlström, Rod Andrew, Henri Bérenger, Bob Buchanan, Bob Chapman, Adrian Coulthard, Nick Craig, Daniel Dahon, Alistair Deaves, Tim Edwards, Ralph Eriksen, Mark Gardner, Christophe Gaugier, Thomas Hansson-Mild, Wietze Huitema, Mark Jackson, Peter Jackson, Svend Jakobsen, Henry Metcalfe, Richard Morell, Fritz Mueller, Mike Patton, Norbert Petrausch, Jean-Pierre Gailes, François Podevyn, Jörg Rademacher, Mary Reddyhoff, Karen Robertson, Bob Ross, Peter Scheuerl, Thorsten Schmidt, Jonty Sherwill, Rodney Thorne, Bill Tyler, Jan Tyler, Leanne Tyler, Per Westlund, Grant Wakefield, Sten Waldö, Greg Wilcox, and anyone else who helped...

Printed in Great Britain
by Amazon